D0886676

The Florida Water Story
From Raindrops to the Sea

by Peggy S. Lantz and Wendy A. Hale

Illustrations by Jean Barnes

Table of Contents

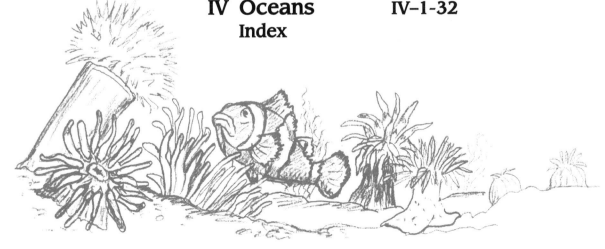

DEDICATION

To my mother, who first taught me to love the written word. —Peggy Lantz

To Nikki and Chris, and our family's love of the sea. —Wendy Hale

To Mikey and in memory of Ruth E. and Albert G. Wilson.—Jean Barnes

INTRODUCTION

Florida is blessed with water. Water makes the difference between desert and flourishing green plants, as much of the land around the earth at the same latitude as Florida is desert.

Clouds that gather constantly over the Gulf of Mexico and the Atlantic Ocean blow inland over Florida and drop rain at an average annual rate of an inch a week.

The flatness of the land, while it may seem monotonous to visitors from mountainous areas, is a blessing for retaining water. In mountainous and hilly regions, the water runs off rapidly. In Florida, rivers flow slowly, soaking the land as they go. The great "river of grass"—the Everglades—flows only one mile an hour. Shallow "bowls" all over the state retain water for plants, birds, and other animals.

This book is about Florida's water—its springs and rivers, lakes and wetlands, bays, and the seas around it—where it comes from and where it goes, who lives in it and around it, and what humans are doing to it.

Text copyright © 1998 by Peggy S. Lantz and Wendy A. Hale
Illustrations copyright © 1998 by Jean Barnes

All rights reserved. No part of this book may be reproduced in any form or by any means, electronic or mechanical, including photocopying, recording, or by any information storage and retrieval system, without permission in writing from the publisher.

Inquiries should be addressed to:
Pineapple Press, Inc.
P.O. Box 3899
Sarasota, Florida 34230

First Edition
10 9 8 7 6 5 4 3 2 1

Design by Carol Tornatore
Layout by Sandy Wright
Printed and bound by Edwards Brothers, Ann Arbor, Michigan

Library of Congress Cataloging in Publication Data
Lantz, Peggy S.
   The Florida Water Story : From Raindrops to the Sea/by Peggy Sias Lantz and Wendy A. Hale.—1st ed.
     p.   cm.
   Includes index.
   Summary: Follows the water cycle through four major Florida habitats, wetlands, oceans, coastlines, and coral reefs.
    ISBN 1-56164-099-9 (alk. paper)
    1. Aquatic ecology—Florida—Juvenile literature. 2. Hydrologic cycle—Florida—Juvenile literature. 3. Water—Florida—Juvenile literature. [1. Hydrologic cycle—Florida. 2. Aquatic ecology—Florida. 3. Ecology—Florida.] I. Hale, Wendy, 1954–. II. Title.
QH105.F6L356   1998
551.48'09759—dc21
    97-45043
CIP
AC

Wetlands

*f*resh water makes Florida a land of rivers, shining lakes and green leaves, colorful flowers, and many different kinds of natural places. The rain that falls on this bright world gathers and flows and winds across the land and drains through its sandy soils. Whether it stands on the ground or seeps into it, runs off in rivers or stays in swamps, gathers into ponds or flows in a broad sheet, water makes special places for plants and animals to live. We invite you to come with us as we explore the many different wet places of Florida—from the falling raindrops to the sea's edge.

Water Cycle

The water that laps at Florida's shores, that rains on its trees and houses, that wanders down its rivers to the ocean, and that bubbles up from its underground aquifers is all part of the planet's water cycle. All the water on earth recycles continually. It precipitates as rain from the sky onto the land and the ocean. On land it percolates down into the sand, evaporates from lakes and wetlands, or transpires from plants. Then the water vapor rises up again where it condenses into clouds in the sky.

Most water on earth is salty ocean. Only a very small part is fresh, drinkable water, and most of that is trapped in ice at the North and South Poles. The tiny fraction that's left over provides fresh water to all living things.

Florida is blessed with fresh water. Though the state is surrounded by salty seas, the clouds that gather moisture over the ocean are made up of fresh water. Rain falls abundantly on this beautiful green state, often dropped in thunderstorms. Because Florida has no mountains and few hills, its flat surface keeps water on the land rather than allowing it to run rapidly to the sea.

condensation

precipitation

lake

percolation

aquifer

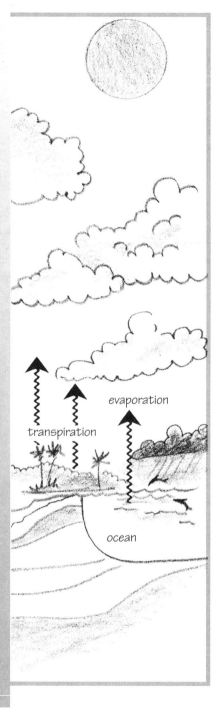

evaporation

transpiration

ocean

aquifer   water in an underground layer of sand or rock.
condensation   changing from water vapor to liquid water.
evaporation   changing from a liquid to a vapor.

percolation   trickling downward through the soil.
precipitation   water that falls to earth (in Florida, as rain or hail, rarely as snow).
transpiration   giving off water vapor through leaves.

Florida's Seasons

Florida is a long state. Plants and animals that can live in the cooler areas of north Florida are different from those that can live in the warmer areas of south Florida. But the difference between summer and winter is more a matter of rain than of temperature. The summer rains and the winter dry spell mark the seasons. These wet and dry seasons are important to Florida's plant and animal life.

Walking on water
Coots and common moorhens walk on top of water lily pads. Their long toes spread their weight over the lily pad. They turn the pads over to find insects, frogs, spiders, and algae to eat.

The long and short of it
Plants and animals adapt to the rise and fall of water levels. White water lilies grow long stems—up to 3 or 4 meters (10 or 12 feet)—when the summer rains come and the water rises, so that the pads and flowers can float on the surface.

algae   certain plants that usually live in water.

"Old Baldy"

Bald cypress trees grow in wet places, and mature trees can live on flooded land. Seedlings and young trees, however, need regular changes in the water level to survive, because they cannot stand constant flooding. A cypress tree spreads wide at the base of its trunk to keep it stable in soggy soil. It sprouts tall growths on its roots called knees that scientists think help the tree absorb oxygen when the water is deep. It's called bald because it loses its tiny leaves in the winter.

Pretty, but shy

The moorhen's gorgeous but shy cousin, the purple gallinule, needs especially good hiding cover. It lives among thickly growing water plants such as willows and cattails.

Wading birds nest during the dry season so that, as ponds shrink, the fish they feed on are crowded together, making them easier to catch for hungry nestlings.

Old Ironhead

The wood stork is one of the wading birds that uses the rise and fall of the water to its advantage. It is an endangered species that nests in large colonies in bald cypress trees or mangrove trees. It is a very large white bird, up to 1 meter (40 inches) tall, with black wing tips and tail. Its featherless gray head gives it nick-names such as ironhead and flinthead. The wood stork feeds by groping around in the muddy water with its bill partly open. When the bill touches prey, it snaps shut.

Good ol' boy

Alligators help other wildlife during long dry periods. When marshes, ponds, and water holes begin drying up, fish, frogs, and many birds and mammals must search for deeper water. An alligator, in satisfying its own need for a water hole, will fling mud and plants out of a small pond with its tail and body, enlarging the refuge for other animals, who may move right in with it.

mammal   an animal that has a backbone and hair, and that gives birth and cares for its young.
prey   an animal that is eaten by another animal.
species   a kind of plant or animal.

Where the Water Goes

Much of the water that rains on Florida trickles slowly down through the sand and is stored in the Floridan aquifer, usually far underground.

Some of it stands in murky swamps or spreads out in flat marshy prairies and floodplains alongside rivers.

Sometimes springs of water bubble out of the aquifer through holes in the limestone.

floodplains   broad, flat areas along a river that become flooded when the river overflows.

Floridan aquifer   Florida's largest underground water storage.

Some of it travels slowly across the miles of Everglades in a broad sheet that moves southward to Florida Bay.

Some of it runs down lazy rivers to the Gulf of Mexico or the Atlantic Ocean.

Some of the water is held in Florida's many shallow, freshwater lakes.

Florida's Rain Barrels

Beneath Florida's sandy soil lies a base of limestone—a porous, spongy-looking, crumbly, yellowish rock that holds water. Florida has more underground water than any other state.

Rainwater falling on the ground soaks rapidly through the spaces between the grains of sand at the surface. It accumulates in holes in the limestone, sometimes within a few feet of the surface and sometimes hundreds of feet below.

These underground water supplies, known as groundwater, are Florida's aquifers. They are filled up mostly by rain, except for a few areas in the Panhandle that are fed by runoff from rivers that begin in the mountains of Georgia.

In some places a layer of clay lies between the sand and the limestone. The fine grains of clay hold the water, allowing it to pass through very slowly or not at all.

In swamps and marshes, water stands for a long time, often drying up only during times of drought. A layer of packed, almost waterproof soil called hardpan may lie under swampy areas.

Sandy soils that allow the rain to seep into the aquifer faster than it does through clay or hardpan are known as recharge areas. Many of these sandy areas occur down the center of the state.

drought   a long period of weeks or months with no rain.
groundwater   water in underground aquifers.
hardpan   a layer of hard-packed soil that water cannot easily go through.

porous   having pores, or holes, through which water can flow.
recharge areas   places where sandy soil lets water seep through to the aquifer.

I-8

The Floridan Aquifer

The biggest aquifer under the state, called "Florida's rain barrel," is the Floridan aquifer. Its water is pure and sweet.

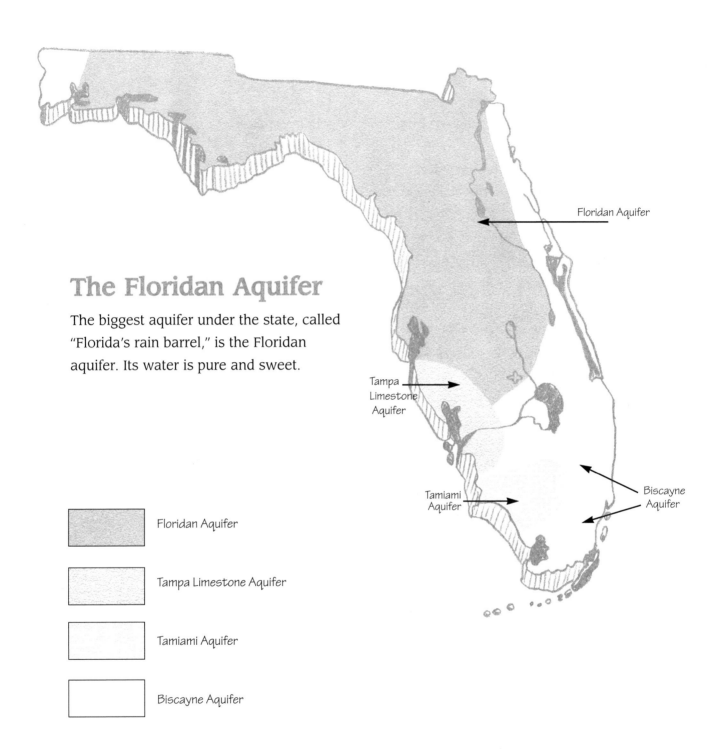

Floridan Aquifer

Tampa Limestone Aquifer

Tamiami Aquifer

Biscayne Aquifer

Springs

Springs occur where groundwater, held under pressure in the limestone, finds a crack and bubbles up through a natural hole in the rock. Florida has hundreds of springs. Twenty-seven of them are called first-magnitude springs, which discharge more than 227 million liters (60 million gallons) of water each day.

Spring water is usually pure and clear. It comes up from deep in the earth, where air temperature doesn't affect it, at a constant year-round temperature of around 22 degrees C (72 degrees F).

Water overflows from the springs and runs toward the sea. Tiny springs bubble up through the sand in many of Florida's rivers. Even seepages—where water oozes out of the ground, usually after a rainy summer—are evidence of Florida's wonderful supply of groundwater.

A hole in the ground
An artesian well is a kind of spring. It is not natural, however, because the hole through the rock is made with a drill by someone searching for water to drink or to irrigate a garden or farm. When the drill strikes water under pressure, water shoots out the top of the well pipe. It can continue to bubble out of the pipe for years.

Look out for the claws!
Crayfish look like tiny lobsters. Raccoons eat them and will stand at the edge of the spring, turning over waterlogged branches or feeling under roots to search for them.

Sea Cows

Though spring water feels cold to human swimmers, it is warm enough to be life-saving for the West Indian manatee, an endangered aquatic mammal. In summer, manatees swim throughout the Caribbean Sea, the Gulf of Mexico, and part of the Atlantic Ocean. But in the winter months, as the water in the ocean and lagoons becomes colder, many manatees come to Florida and swim up the rivers to seek out the warmer water near springs. Manatees need water warmer than 18 degrees C (65 degrees F) to stay alive.

The manatee, sometimes called a sea cow because it eats grasses and other plants, is nearly as big as a cow. It feeds under water, but must rise to the surface to breathe every three to five minutes. Manatees move slowly, and many of them carry scars from cuts made by motorboat propellers.

Few manatees are born each year because a female gives birth to only a single calf, which stays with its mother until it is two years old.

Scientists believe that only about 2,000 manatees still exist in Florida.

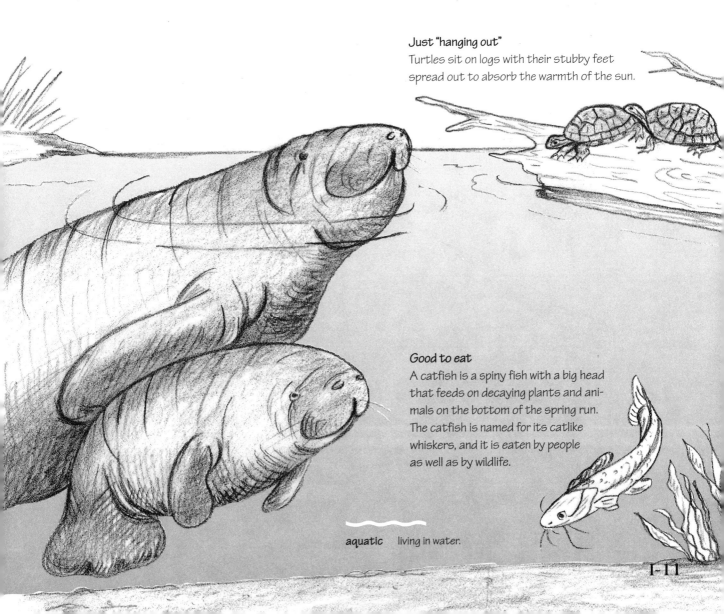

Just "hanging out"
Turtles sit on logs with their stubby feet spread out to absorb the warmth of the sun.

Good to eat
A catfish is a spiny fish with a big head that feeds on decaying plants and animals on the bottom of the spring run. The catfish is named for its catlike whiskers, and it is eaten by people as well as by wildlife.

aquatic   living in water.

I-11

Rivers

A fast way for water to get from aquifers to the sea is by a river, even when it's a sluggish, slow-moving Florida river.

Some Florida rivers rise out of the ground in big bubbling springs.

Other rivers gather from swamps, marshes, and ponds until they find a channel to the sea.

Some flow out of a lake.

In Florida's Panhandle, the Apalachicola River arises in the hills of Georgia, where it collects melted snow as well as rainfall.

Many of Florida's rivers are dark-colored because of brown stain from plants. They are called blackwater rivers. The rivers that run from springs, however, usually flow shining clear. Where blackwater streams meet clear rivers, their mingled waters turn dark.

Because Florida rivers flow slowly, canoeists can easily paddle against the current on most of them, but in a few places where limestone rocks are near the surface, the river will offer some whitewater to canoeists.

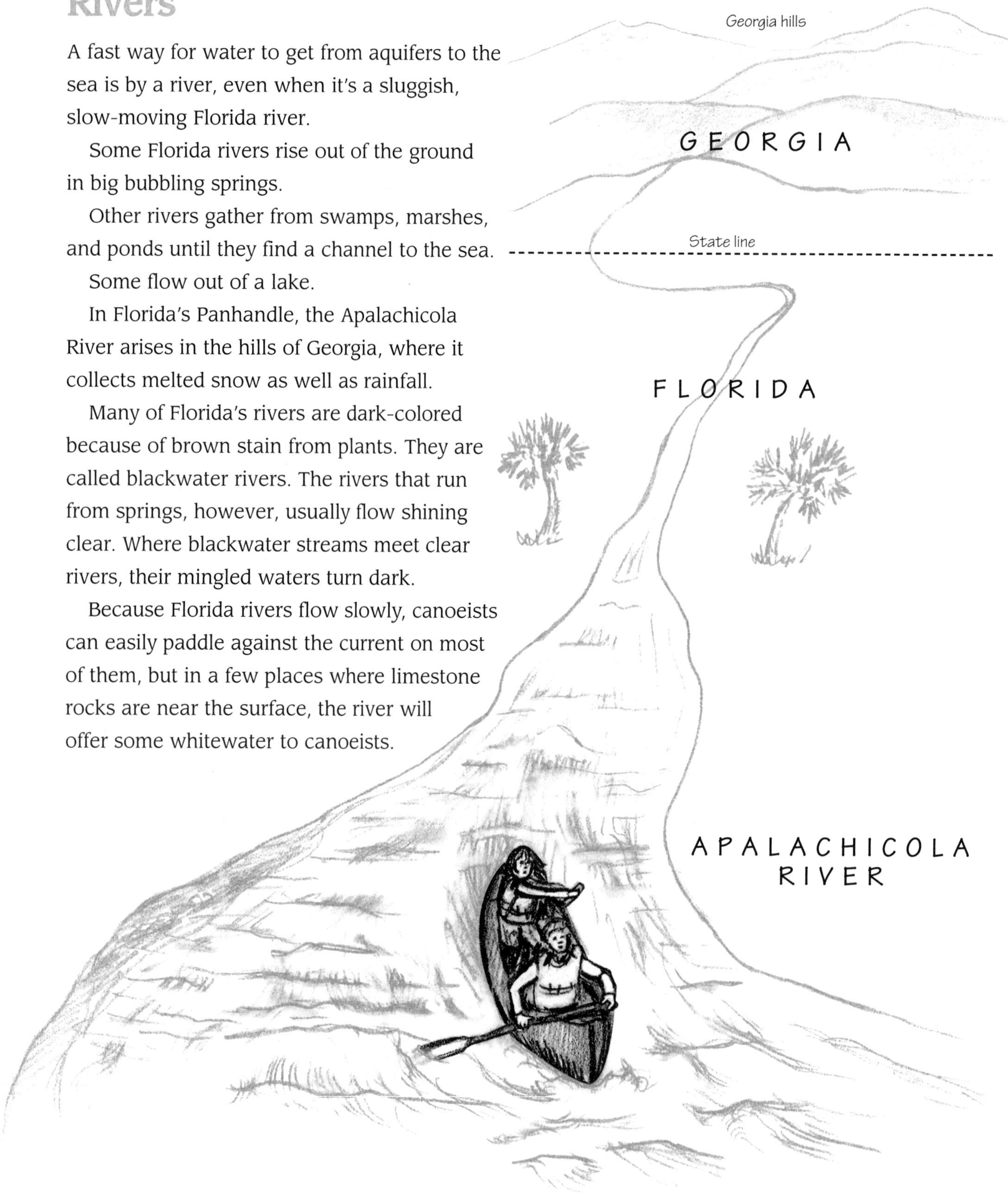

Georgia hills

G E O R G I A

State line

F L O R I D A

A P A L A C H I C O L A
R I V E R

whitewater   *frothy water caused by rocks.*

The snail kite

This bird of prey has sharp talons and a sharp, curved beak, just right for prying snails out of their shells. Apple snails are its major food. It snatches the snails out of the water as it flies, then perches to eat. The male is slate gray with red legs; the female is brown. It is endangered and lives mostly in the southern half of Florida.

An apple for the birds

Apple snails, which may grow to about the size of golf balls, climb up the stalks of water plants and lay their small, pinkish eggs above the water's surface. Here the snails develop inside the eggs and out of reach of fish that might eat them. Later, the tiny snails hatch and drop into the water.

The limpkin

This rare, brown bird with white spots wades along the edges of rivers, poking its curved bill into the mud or water for apple snails or sometimes small crabs or worms. It makes a noisy, croaking call.

bird of prey   a bird with curved beak and sharp talons that kills and eats other animals.
talons   the sharp, curved claws of a bird of prey.

Fuel Stop

Wetlands along rivers are important habitats for migrating songbirds that stop to feed on their way south in the fall and north in the spring. Some species stay in Florida to raise their families.

Spring and fall colors

Red maple trees provide color to Florida's wetlands in fall and spring. The leaves turn red when days become shorter, and the new leaves, blossoms, and seeds are bright red in the spring.

Woody's friend

A pileated woodpecker is a large, black-and-white woodpecker with a bright red crest. This bird was the inspiration for the cartoon bird, Woody Woodpecker. If you are nearby, you might hear one whacking its beak on a rotting tree stump in a search for beetles or carpenter ants to eat.

Animal hotel

River wetlands often have dead trees where woodpeckers build their nesting holes. When the woodpecker is through raising its family, the hole may be used by other animals, such as raccoons, opossums, and screech owls.

migrating   moving from one place to another with the seasons.

The Everglades, River of Grass

The Everglades is a land of many different habitats. It is a broad, shallow river. It is a wet prairie. It is a freshwater marsh. It has islands called hammocks, where rare trees grow to champion size and common trees grow thick and green.

And it is huge. A hundred years ago, it flowed in a 160-kilometer-wide (100-mile-wide) sheet of water just a dozen centimeters (a few inches) deep all the way from Lake Okeechobee to Florida Bay, a distance of nearly 160 kilometers.

Now, however, after many ditches and canals have been dug, the Everglades is less than half its former size, and the water flow is controlled by people instead of nature.

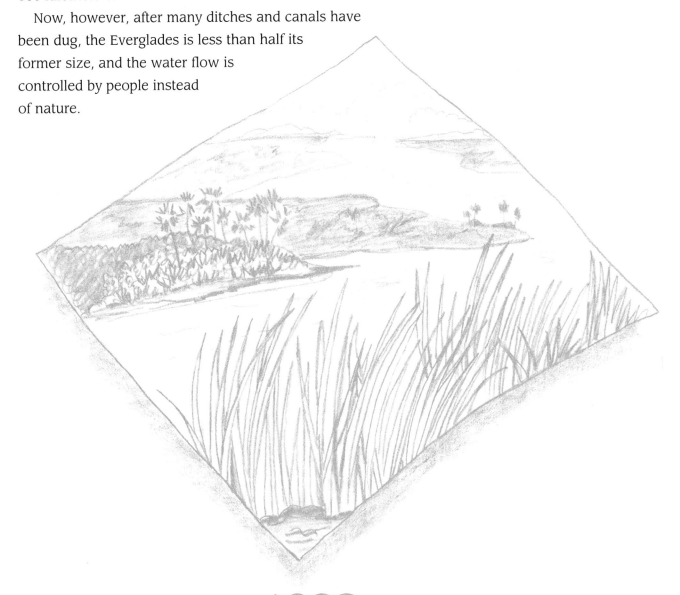

habitat   the place where a plant or animal naturally grows and lives.
hammock   slightly higher ground, where many trees grow, in a wetland.

The Everglades, as it was before and still is now, is a strange, forbidding, watery land, unique in all the world. In the 1800s, the Seminole Indians hid in the Everglades to escape the U.S. Army. The Indians called this land Pa-hay-o-kee, meaning "grassy waters."

Ouch!

Sawgrass covers most of the remaining Everglades. It is a grasslike plant that grows from knee-high to taller than an adult. It looks similar to cattails, but has spiny leaf edges that can tear skin and clothing.

Slow motion color

Tree snails are about as big as Ping-Pong balls and have colorful, striped shells. They live on tree branches in the hammocks of the Everglades and the Keys, and they eat tiny fungi and algae that grow on bark and leaves.

fungi   plants that are not green, such as mushrooms.

A chain of food

Periphyton is a pale yellow-green algae that grows under water in mats. It forms the bottom of the food chain in the Everglades. Microscopic plants and animals hide in and feed on the periphyton. These microscopic plants and animals are eaten by insects and other small organisms, which are then eaten by fish and small animals, which in turn become the food of larger fish, birds, and frogs. At the top of this food chain is the alligator, the king of the Everglades, which feeds on the larger animals.

food chain   the passage of food energy from plants, which make their own food from the energy of the sun, to animals that eat plants, to animals that eat other animals.
microscopic   too small to be seen without a magnifying lens.
organisms   living plants and animals.

The Alligator

The American alligator lives in all of Florida's wet habitats, from the Panhandle to the Everglades. It is the largest reptile in the United States (along with the American crocodile, which lives in salty water only at the southern tip of Florida).

Like all reptiles, the alligator is cold-blooded, which means that its body temperature adjusts to the temperature of the air, water, sunshine, and soil touching it. When the weather is warm, the alligator is active. When cold, it searches for a warm, sunny spot or becomes inactive, often burying itself in the mud under water. It must rise to the surface to breathe, but can stay under water for hours, especially if its body is cold.

A female alligator builds a nest out of plants that she piles in a mound about a meter (3 feet) high. She lays 30 to 50 eggs, which are as big as hens' eggs, inside the mound in early summer. As the plants decay, the pile heats up and keeps the eggs warm. The mother alligator stays nearby to protect her eggs from predators such as raccoons, bears, and otters. In about 70 days, the baby alligators inside the eggs begin cheeping. The mother digs them out as they hatch and carries them in her mouth a few at a time to the water. She then protects the hatchlings from raccoons or wading birds.

predator   an animal that kills and eats other animals.

Do Not Feed the Alligators!

When people feed alligators, or any wild animals, the animals tend to lose their fear of humans. Then they may come close to people swimming or even enter backyards, looking for a handout. It is against the law to feed alligators.

Sinkholes

Florida is pockmarked with sinkholes. Like its lakes, some sinkholes are deep, some are broad and shallow. Some hold water, some are dry. Many of them are hundreds or thousands of years old. Sinkholes are created when water eats away the limestone underground. The surface of the ground either sinks slowly into the hollow caused by the eroding limestone, or it suddenly collapses when the rock roof of an underground cavern caves in.

The collapse of a sinkhole can be spectacular. It may happen during a dry period when the water level drops, leaving an underground cave with no water in it to help hold up the roof, which then falls in. Or it may happen during a rainy period when the soil on the roof of the cave becomes so heavy with water that it collapses the roof.

Sinkholes can occur anywhere in the state, any time of the year.

A cool hideaway

Sinkholes provide cool, moist habitats that provide shelter for some special plants and animals. Inside, they are protected from fires and drying winds. Water often seeps through the walls, helping to maintain a nearly constant temperature year-round.

Mosses and ferns often cling to the slopes of sinkholes. Carolina wrens and tufted titmice sometimes nest in sinkholes, and snakes, lizards, frogs, and insects take refuge in them.

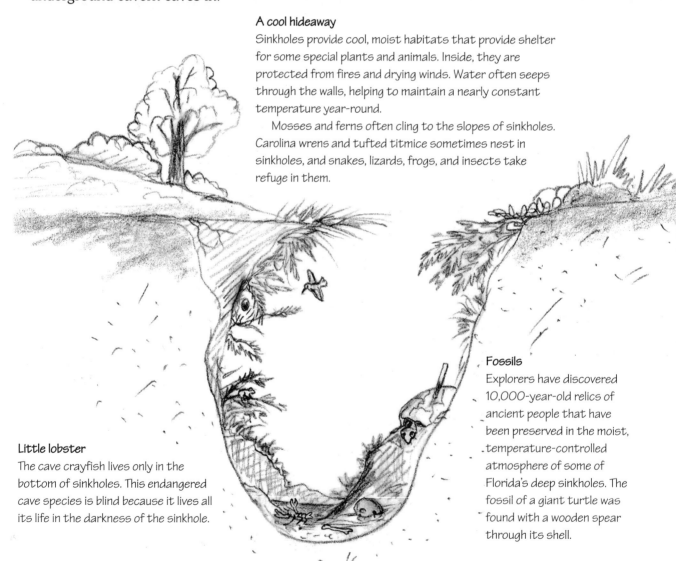

Little lobster

The cave crayfish lives only in the bottom of sinkholes. This endangered cave species is blind because it lives all its life in the darkness of the sinkhole.

Fossils

Explorers have discovered 10,000-year-old relics of ancient people that have been preserved in the moist, temperature-controlled atmosphere of some of Florida's deep sinkholes. The fossil of a giant turtle was found with a wooden spear through its shell.

fossil   a mineralized piece of a plant or animal from a past age. *Mineralized* means that, over a long time, hard nonliving material replaces soft living material.

relic   a surviving piece of a past civilization.

Lakes and Ponds

Florida has more than 7,000 lakes of all sizes. Many of them are sinkhole lakes.

Lakes in Florida vary. They can be small and shallow, large and shallow, or small and deep, but none of them are large and deep. Most are between 2 and 6 meters (7 and 20 feet) deep. Many grassy ponds are only knee-deep and may dry up in the winter.

Some lakes are clear, with sandy bottoms, reflecting blue sky and clouds. Some are stained brown by tree leaves and roots. Some are green with algae. Some are surrounded by bald cypress trees.

Some are covered with white water lily pads or cattails. Grasses, purple-flowered pickerelweed, and white-flowered arrowhead plants may grow in the shallow water around the edges. Many kinds of fish, frogs, and insects hatch and live among the plants.

Wet and dry seasons contribute to the rise and fall of these shallow lakes, which are usually filled by heavy summer rains and lowered by evaporation between rains and during the dry winter.

The bird with patches
The red-winged blackbird is known for its glossy black feathers and red and yellow shoulder patches. The female, which is dark brown with a striped breast, builds her woven-grass nest in a thick stand of cattails, tying it to cattail leaves for support.

Dip and dabble
Ducks that come to Florida for the winter find grass-edged Florida lakes a haven from the cold northern winters. They dip and dabble in the shallow water to feed on algae, aquatic insects, or underwater plants.

Tadpoles to frogs

Sometimes in spring you can see schools of tadpoles in the shallow waters of lakes. They hatch from eggs laid in a greenish, jellylike blob in the water. A tadpole may be about the size of a pea—with a tail. It feeds on microscopic creatures in the mud and water. As it grows, its tail shrinks, and hind legs and forelegs develop. When it has four legs and almost no tail, it can emerge from the water as an adult frog with air-breathing lungs instead of gills.

A frog is an amphibian, which means it begins its life in the water as a tadpole with gills, but it breathes air when it becomes an adult. A frog has a long, sticky tongue, which it zaps out to capture insects to eat.

Peepers

Tree frogs are the most numerous of the frogs. They live high in trees, eat insects, and sing in loud choruses at night. Spring peepers are especially vocal, and get their name from their high-pitched "peeping" sound.

Finny Things

Florida lakes and rivers are full of fish of many kinds.

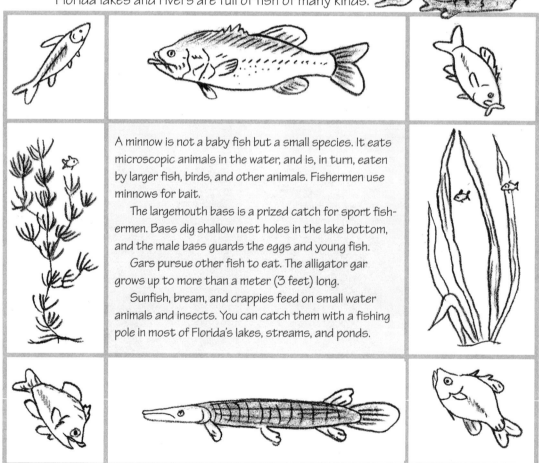

A minnow is not a baby fish but a small species. It eats microscopic animals in the water, and is, in turn, eaten by larger fish, birds, and other animals. Fishermen use minnows for bait.

The largemouth bass is a prized catch for sport fishermen. Bass dig shallow nest holes in the lake bottom, and the male bass guards the eggs and young fish.

Gars pursue other fish to eat. The alligator gar grows up to more than a meter (3 feet) long.

Sunfish, bream, and crappies feed on small water animals and insects. You can catch them with a fishing pole in most of Florida's lakes, streams, and ponds.

The Osprey and the Eagle
Two Fish-eating Birds of Prey

Fish hawk

The osprey dives for its fish from high in the air, plunging into the water feet-first. It builds its nest in the top of a dead snag or a living tree near a river, a lake, or the coast. Because of the osprey's white head, many people think they are seeing a bald eagle, but the osprey has a dark tail and white breast. The eagle has a white tail as well as a white head, and the rest of its body is dark.

Our national bird

More bald eagles live in Florida than any other state in the U.S. except Alaska. The bald eagle needs wetlands because its primary food is fish. An eagle snatches fish from the water with its talons as it flies over a lake, or sometimes steals fish from another bird.

Eagles mate for life, and the pair builds a big nest in the top of a tall pine or cypress tree near water. The nest is often added to and reused year after year.

Wading Birds

Florida's beautiful wading birds are large and colorful, with long legs and long necks. The shallow depths of Florida's lakes and ponds aid wading birds in their search for food. Differences in their size, bill shape, and choice of food make it possible for several species to feed together in the same pond. But each of them must juggle the catch around in its beak until it can swallow the fish headfirst so the fins won't catch in its throat.

Herons, egrets, and wood storks build their nests and lay their eggs as the winter dry season begins. By the time their eggs have hatched, water levels are beginning

The biggest
The great blue heron is the largest of Florida's wading birds, standing over a meter (about 4 feet) tall. It is also one of the most easily seen, for it doesn't seem to mind being watched. It is blue-gray with a white head and a long, tan neck streaked with black.

During breeding season, its colors are bright, and long, wispy feathers flow from its head and back. A great blue heron stands still in the water while hunting, waiting for a fish, frog, or lizard to pass within reach of its strike.

An all-white variety of this bird, sometimes called the great white heron, is found in south Florida and the Keys. Its bill and legs are yellow.

More wading birds

The little blue heron is all white or mottled blue-and-white before it grows its dark blue adult feathers. It stalks slowly through shallow water after fish or frogs.

The snowy egret is recognized by its black bill and black legs with "yellow slippers." It strides through the water after frogs, fish, and many other kinds of aquatic organisms, including insects.

The green heron hunches on a branch over the water until a minnow swims by. Then it stabs downward to catch the fish without letting go of the branch.

The tricolored heron sometimes chases its prey through the water, zig-zagging after a fleeing fish.

I-24

to fall in lakes, marshes, and swamps. Fish that have been growing and multiplying in the deeper waters during the summer wet season are now crowded together in slowly drying ponds. Sometimes they are trapped in small puddles, making it even easier for birds to catch fish for their hungry nestlings.

Most of the wading birds can be seen in many different habitats everywhere in Florida. They roost and nest in large flocks, but usually hunt for their meals alone. They nest near and feed in the shallow waters of marshes, wet prairies, swamps, lakes, and ponds.

Loves company

White ibis are often seen in flocks when feeding as well as when roosting or nesting. They poke their long, red, down-curved bills in soft mud along riverbanks, lake edges, and wet prairies searching for aquatic insects, crayfish, crabs, and grasshoppers.

Common, American, White, and Great

The great egret has had many name changes, at one time or another known officially by all of these. It is not quite as tall as the great blue heron, and is gleaming white except for its yellow bill and dark legs. Sometimes it enters backyard habitats and becomes relatively tame. It stalks stiff-legged and slowly after fish in marshes and along lake edges.

Swamps

Swamps are wet, wooded places where water sometimes stands for much of the year. Only to humans are they dark and creepy. For the plants and animals that live there, swamps are quiet, safe places.

Swamps have many different names. They may be called strands, sloughs, estuaries, bogs, domes, bayheads, or bottomlands.

The main feature of a swamp is soil that is saturated, or heavy, with water. A layer of hardpan, peat, or heavy clay soil prevents water from trickling quickly downward to the aquifer. Swamps have water a few centimeters to a meter or more (a few feet) deep for at least part of the year. Streams of deeper water often flow slowly through swamps.

During Florida's summer rainy season, thunderstorms and sometimes hurricanes drop many centimeters of water on the land. Because swamps are lower than the surrounding land, they can store large amounts of water from higher ground during storms.

Air plants

Some plants do not grow in soil but survive on moisture and dust in the air. They are called air plants, and many of them grow on trees in moist, shady swamps. Some orchids are air plants. Wild pine is a type of air plant that has stiff, pointed leaves that look like the top of a pineapple.

Spanish moss is an air plant, too. It does not harm the tree it hangs on and can even live on telephone wires.

Swamp flowers

Orchids are among the most beautiful of flowers. Many of them live in swamps where they often cling to the branches of cypress and swamp bay trees, and where it rarely gets cold.

Many orchids have descriptive names, such as ghost orchid (the rarest), clamshell orchid, and butterfly orchid (the most common).

Woodies

The male wood duck is the most colorful and beautiful of all ducks. This shy bird prefers the seclusion of swamps where it stays hidden among grape vines, swamp lilies, fallen tree branches, and stumps.

The female "woodie" lays up to 20 eggs in a dead tree with a hole in it, preferably near water. A month later, the ducklings hatch. When they are only a day old, the mother duck leaves the nest, coaxing them to jump out of the nest and flutter to the water, sometimes several meters (many feet) below.

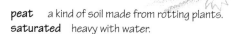

peat   a kind of soil made from rotting plants.
saturated   heavy with water.

Kites

The swallow-tailed kite has a long, forked tail and black-and-white feathers. It may nest in a tall cypress or pine tree in a Florida swamp. It is a bird of prey, catching grasshoppers, dragonflies, lizards, and small snakes and eating them while still flying.

An endangered fern

The hand fern is a small, endangered fern shaped like a person's hand. It grows only in deep swamps in the boots of cabbage palm trees, with its fingerlike leaves hanging downward.

Night-owls

The barred owl is a bird of the swamps. One of its nicknames is swamp owl, though it can be found in other habitats, too. It calls at night with a loud "who-cooks-for-you-all," and sometimes it fills the woods with hysterical cries. It eats rodents such as rats, mice, and squirrels, and nests in a tree during the winter.

B'ars

The Florida black bear lives in swamps and other dense habitats. It is mostly vegetarian, eating all kinds of fruits and berries, but it also eats ants, beetles, and other insects, and occasionally birds and mammals. It needs many square kilometers (miles) of land to roam in.

boots   the stubs of broken fronds that still cling to the cabbage palm tree.

Marshes and Prairies

Marshes and prairies are wide, grassy, treeless places with peaty, wet soil. They often surround swamps or lakes or occur along the edges of rivers. Water from rainfall stands on them part of the year.

Some of the birds and mammals that live in the marshes build their nests just above water level—high enough to avoid drowning their babies, but low enough to protect them from predators by a moat of water around their nests.

Some plants do not live on nutrients from soil, water, or even air. They eat insects, and they are called carnivorous. Most species of carnivorous plants are found in the bogs of north Florida and the Panhandle.

Come into my parlor
Pitcher plants have tube-shaped stalks with hoods over the top of the stalk. Insects are attracted by these colorful hoods or the sweet nectar inside. When they land on the slippery edge of the stalk, they fall inside and can't crawl back out because the stalk is lined with hairs that point downward. Eventually they drown and are digested by the plant's juices.

Bunnies
The marsh rabbit lives in the wet prairies of Florida. It has a brown tail instead of the white tuft of the cottontail rabbit, and its large feet help it walk on soggy ground. It is an expert swimmer and diver, and escapes predators by taking to deep water. It eats grasses and aquatic plants.

bog   a name for a swamp.
carnivorous   feeding on animals.
nutrients   foods that promote growth.

Sandies

The sandhill crane is a very large bird that builds its nest on the prairies of Florida. It eats both plants and insects. Sometimes its nest floats when the water rises after a rainstorm. If it finds no wet places in the prairie, it will not raise a family.

Danger!

The dangerous cottonmouth, or water moccasin, one of Florida's poisonous snakes, lives in many wet places, including wet prairies. It will capture and eat almost any animal that is small enough for it to swallow, even small marsh rabbits.

Big cat

The Florida panther spends some of its life in wetlands, because here is where it can often find its preferred prey, the white-tailed deer. The panther, large and tawny-colored, is Florida's most endangered animal.

Fire

Did you know that fires help Florida's wetlands? Fires that happen naturally are started by lightning, usually when summer thunderstorms begin but while the winter-killed grasses and leaves are still dry. Some hardwood trees will be killed by a fire, but other plants benefit.

After a fire, a good rain will cause everything to sprout and grow greener and healthier than before. Insects, birds, and mammals will return to the burned area to take advantage of the tasty new growth.

Standing water in swamps and prairies will cause a fire to burn in patches around the water, leaving a variety of different habitats for different species of plants and animals. These habitats also will change gradually over the years, depending upon how often fire burns through.

The Value of Florida's Wetlands

All of Florida's wetland habitats are important to people, yet we've been draining, diking, and ditching them for a hundred years, thinking they were worthless.

Before development of wetlands began, water covered more than half of Florida. By the end of the twentieth century, people had reduced that to about a fifth of the state.

Wetlands hold and slowly release water. Without them, Florida could become a desert. Wetlands also cleanse and purify water. Without them, Florida's water could become unsafe to drink. Many of Florida's wild plants and animals need the wetlands to live in or they will become endangered.

People have taken a long time to realize the benefits of Florida's many and varied wetlands. We must learn to appreciate and protect these important natural areas, not just for the plants and animals that live in them, but for the people who live in Florida.

Glossary

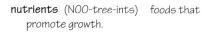

algae (AL-jee)   certain plants that usually live in water.

aquatic (uh-KWAHT-ik)   living in water.

aquifer (AK-wi-fur)   water in an underground layer of sand or rock.

bird of prey   a bird with curved beak and sharp talons that kills and eats other animals.

bog   a name for a swamp.

boots   the stubs of broken fronds that still cling to the cabbage palm tree.

carnivorous (kar-NIV-er-us)   feeding on animals.

condensation   changing from water vapor to liquid water.

drought   a long period of weeks or months with no rain.

evaporation   changing from a liquid to a vapor.

floodplains   broad, flat areas along a river that become flooded when the river overflows.

Floridan aquifer   Florida's largest underground water storage.

food chain   the passage of food energy from plants, which make their own food from the energy of the sun, to animals that eat plants, to animals that eat other animals.

fossil   a mineralized piece of a plant or animal from a past age. *Mineralized* means that, over a long time, hard non-living material replaces soft living material.

fungi (FUN-ji)   plants that are not green, such as mushrooms.

groundwater   water in underground aquifers.

habitat   the place where a plant or animal naturally grows and lives.

hammock   slightly higher ground, where many trees grow, in a wetland.

hardpan   a layer of hard-packed soil that water cannot easily go through.

mammal   an animal that has a backbone and hair, and that gives birth and cares for its young.

microscopic (mi-kro-SCOP-ik)   too small to be seen without a magnifying lens.

migrating   moving from one place to another with the seasons.

nutrients (NOO-tree-ints)   foods that promote growth.

organisms   living plants and animals.

peat   a kind of soil made from rotting plants.

percolation   trickling downward through the soil.

porous   having pores, or holes, through which water can flow.

precipitation   water that falls to earth (in Florida, as rain or hail, rarely as snow).

predator   an animal that kills and eats other animals.

prey   an animal that is eaten by another animal.

recharge areas   places where sandy soil lets water seep through to the aquifer.

relic   a surviving piece of a past civilization.

saturated   heavy with water.

species (SPEE-sheez)   a kind of plant or animal.

talons   the sharp, curved claws of a bird of prey.

transpiration   giving off water vapor through leaves.

whitewater   frothy water caused by rocks.

Coastlines

*f*lorida's coastline is washed by the Atlantic Ocean on the east and the Gulf of Mexico on the west. At its southern tip, between the mainland and the curving string of islands called the Florida Keys, Florida Bay connects these two large seas.

The entire coastline is wrinkled with bays and inlets, lagoons and barrier islands. It is more than 1,800 kilometers (1,100 miles) long—the longest coastline of any state except Alaska.

The edge between land and sea—where fresh waters from springs, swamps, lakes, and rivers reach the salt waters of the oceans—provides many different places, or habitats, for special plants and animals to live. Many of them are unable to live anywhere else. Come explore the beaches, the mangrove forests, and the estuaries, salt marshes, and lagoons of Florida's long coastline.

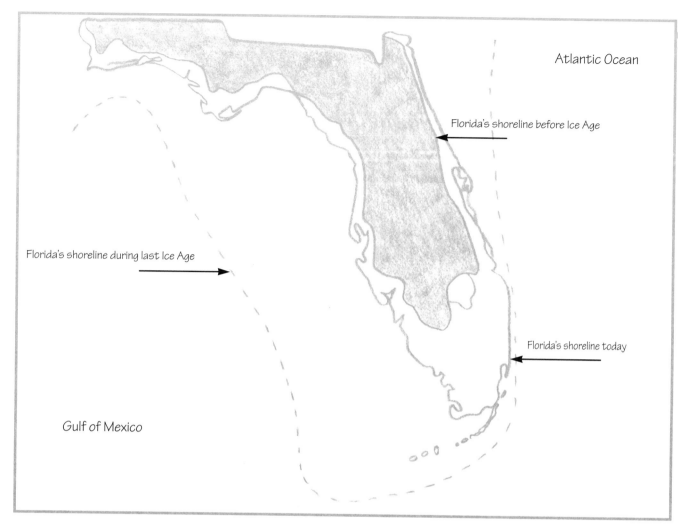

Atlantic Ocean

Florida's shoreline before Ice Age

Florida's shoreline during last Ice Age

Florida's shoreline today

Gulf of Mexico

Florida's Many Shorelines

Millions of years ago, Florida was hardly here at all. A few small islands of the central ridge of what would one day be Florida stuck up out of the ocean. Florida's shoreline was small, because the ocean was bigger. The earth's weather was warm—warm almost to the Arctic Circle—and only a small amount of water was frozen in ice at the North and South Poles.

Then earth's weather became colder. Glaciers and icebergs formed in what is now Canada and the northern United States. The great oceans of the world shrank as their waters became bound up in ice. The water's edge receded around Florida's peninsula, and its shoreline was miles out into what is now the Gulf of Mexico and the Atlantic Ocean.

The Ice Ages came and went four times. Florida grew and shrank four times. The last Ice Age ended about ten thousand years ago. Since then, Florida's shoreline has been about like it is now. We know all this happened because scientists found a whale skeleton far inland and have found artifacts left by humans that are now under water far out in the Gulf of Mexico.

The Cooling of Florida

The huge bodies of water that surround Florida help to keep the state mild and moist. The Atlantic Ocean and the Gulf of Mexico are so huge and deep that the water temperature stays more constant than the land. As the land heats up during the day, the hot air rises, pulling in the cooler air from over the water to replace it. At night, as the land cools below the temperature of the ocean, the breeze blows from the shore toward the water where the warmer air is rising. These pleasant breezes help keep Florida's temperatures—especially south Florida—agreeable year-round.

Clouds gather over ocean and gulf waters, blow across the land, and drop rain often. Especially in the hot summers, thunderheads billow high in the sky, sometimes causing heavy downpours and tornadoes, and making Florida the lightning capital of the United States. Hurricanes begin over the ocean during hot weather and hit Florida's coast more often than any other place in the world.

sea breeze

land breeze

Barrier Islands

Many of the special habitats of Florida's coastline are found on barrier islands—narrow strips of land offshore that run parallel to the coast. Some barrier islands are a few miles long; some are not much bigger than sandbars. They are found along both the Atlantic coast and the Gulf coast of the state.

These islands are constantly changing. Their sands are shifted by winds, waves, tides, and storms. Sometimes during a storm, a small sandbar barrier island disappears and a new one is formed farther along the coast. Or an inlet separating two islands may be filled in or a new inlet opened up.

Barrier islands help protect the mainland of Florida from heavy waves or the storm surge that accompanies a hurricane. They are dangerous places to be when a hurricane is approaching.

Many of Florida's larger barrier islands now are connected to the mainland by bridges and are covered with houses, hotels, and condominiums. Miami Beach is a barrier island. Daytona Beach, Sanibel Island, and Marco Island are all barrier islands. Only a few of the large barrier islands are undeveloped and set aside as seaside parks and wildlife refuges.

barrier islands   narrow strips of land off the coast of Florida or other coastlines that run parallel to the coast.

habitat   a place where a plant or animal naturally grows and lives.

inlet   a narrow waterway opening of the coastline.

offshore   out in the water a distance from the shore.

sandbar   a ridge of sand built up by waves or currents in a body of water.

storm surge   the increased height of the ocean along a coast caused by a hurricane.

The Beach

Besides protecting Florida's coast and providing habitat for wildlife, barrier islands are the places where most of Florida's beautiful beaches are found.

Florida's beaches are known throughout the world for their beautiful white sand. When the tide is out, many of them are broad, hard-packed, and smooth, sloping offshore so gradually that bathers can walk far out into the surf. In the early days of the automobile, the city of Daytona Beach held races on the sand.

The ocean water in Florida is very warm in the summer. But even in the winter, many people from northern states who come to Florida on vacation brave the chillier temperatures to go swimming.

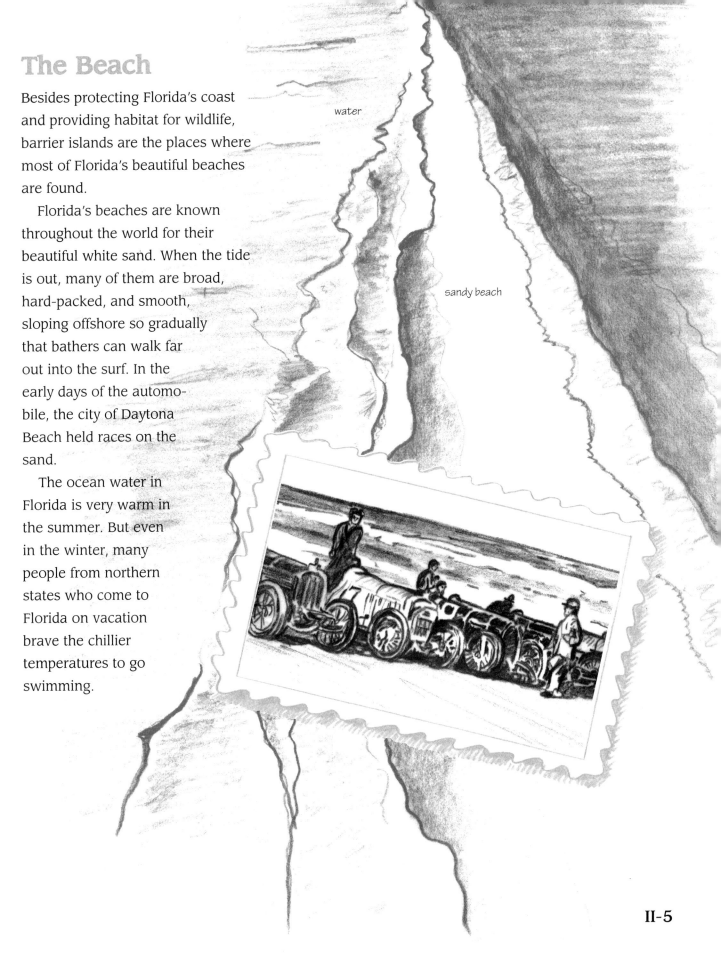

water

sandy beach

Beach Habitats

The beach contains several different habitats, including the lower beach, the middle beach, the upper beach, the dunes, and behind the dunes. The plants and animals that live in these habitats are continuously affected by the ebb and flow of both the waves and the tides.

The Lower Beach

Waves are caused by the wind blowing across the wide sweep of the ocean. As waves approach shallow water and touch bottom, they slow down, and the crests of the waves begin to crowd together. Near the shore, the top of the water begins to move faster than the water below, causing the top water to "break" over the lower water.

The lower part of the beach is under water all the time, with waves crashing and sand churning. This tumbling lower beach is home to animals that burrow in the wet sand. Fish swim in from offshore and birds fly over the waves searching for animals to eat.

Burrowers of the Lower Beach

Money at the beach

The sand dollar is a round, flat animal. When alive, it is covered with short brown spines, but what beachcombers usually find on the beach is its skeleton, bleached white by the sun. It lives in shallow ocean waters, buried just under the sand. If you should find an unbroken sand dollar skeleton, treasure it. If you should find a live sand dollar, leave it alone.

Crabby creature

The mole crab burrows in the fine sand at the edge of the water. Its five pairs of legs are especially shaped for digging, and it digs into the soft sand backwards and very fast. The hard outer shell of the mole crab is about the size and shape of a pecan. Fishermen sometimes call these animals sandbugs and catch them in screened scoops to use for bait to catch fish.

dune   a ridge of sand at the ocean's edge that is piled up by the wind.

ebb and flow   the falling (ebb) and rising (flow) of the tides.

Swimmers of the Lower Beach

Fish, porpoises, and sharks sometimes swim in close to the beach from the deep waters offshore to feed on smaller fish such as mullet, whiting, and pompano that swim close to shore.

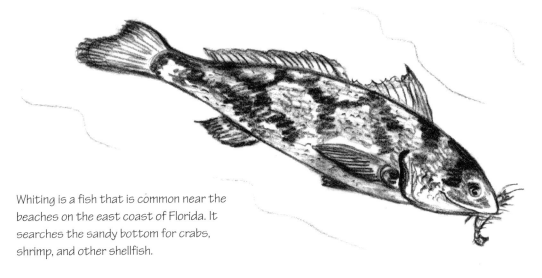

Whiting is a fish that is common near the beaches on the east coast of Florida. It searches the sandy bottom for crabs, shrimp, and other shellfish.

Florida pompano is a fish prized by surf fishermen who stand on the beach and cast their lines into the waves. The pompano's favorite food is mole crabs, and the fish will swim into water as shallow as 9 centimeters (3 inches) deep to search for them.

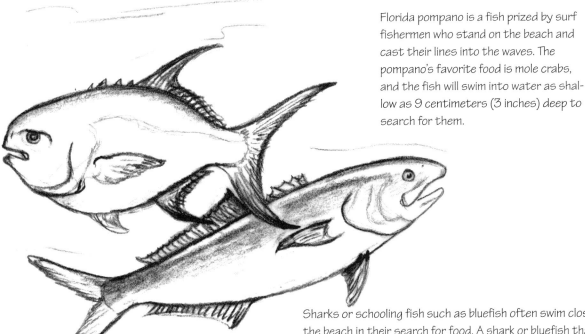

Sharks or schooling fish such as bluefish often swim close to the beach in their search for food. A shark or bluefish that bites a swimmer or surfer near the shore may mistake the person for a fish in the churning breakers.

school   a large number of fish of one species swimming together.
shellfish   an aquatic animal without a skeleton but with a shell.

Gulls are not buoys

Gulls are properly called gulls, not seagulls, for they are found inland just as often as at sea. Several species are common along Florida's coastline all winter, including the herring gull and the ring-billed gull.

They feed on almost everything, from marine creatures and fish (both alive and dead) to picnic leftovers and garbage in landfills. They often rob other birds of their prey or follow fishing boats in large flocks, circling and squabbling for the fish scraps thrown overboard.

Gulls change their plumage many times during their lives as they mature from juvenile to adult and as summer changes to winter. Young gulls may have brown feathers instead of the gray and white of the adults. In winter a gull's black head may turn speckled or gray, and its bill may turn from red to black.

What a funny bird!

The brown pelican is such a large and unusual bird that everyone recognizes it. It is known for its beak-with-a-pouch. Groups of pelicans are often seen flying in lines or V formation above the beach. A pelican fishes in shallow water, diving from 6 to 10 meters (20 to 30 feet) above the waves to scoop up fish in its pouch. When the pelican bobs back to the surface with a catch, water pours out of its pouch, and it juggles its meal until the fish can slide down the bird's throat head first.

Pelicans often nest in huge colonies on mangrove-forested barrier islands, or on islands in lagoons such as Pelican Island in the Indian River. Pelican Island is the nation's first wildlife refuge, set aside by President Theodore Roosevelt in 1903.

Ha, ha, ha

The only gull that nests in Florida and lives here year-round is the laughing gull. It is named for its call, which sounds like chattering laughter. The laughing gull's handsome summertime plumage of black head and red bill and feet make the adult bird easy to identify.

Its nest is usually made of grasses and other dune plants on a sandy barrier island, with three or four eggs laid in May or June.

---

buoy a floating marker tied to the bottom to mark a channel or sandbar for boats.

marine in or about the sea.

plumage the entire covering of feathers on a bird.

prey an animal that is eaten by another animal.

species a kind of plant or animal.

A turn for a tern

Terns have coloring similar to gulls, with white, gray, and black feathers, and often red bills and legs. But terns have more pointed wings than gulls, and some have notched or forked tails, which gulls do not. They never rest on the water as gulls do.

Terns fly high over the waves with their bills pointing downward, sometimes pausing in flight to look for fish. When they spot a meal, they plunge-dive to capture it. Some terns also will feed on crabs or insects.

The scooper skimmer

The black skimmer is a large, ternlike bird with a feature that no other bird has—the lower part of its bill is longer than the upper. It flies just above the water, skimming the waves with its lower bill hanging open, cutting the surface like a scissors. When its lower bill touches a fish or shrimp, the upper bill snaps downward to snatch the prey.

Last and least

The least tern is properly named, for it is the smallest of terns. It is also rare, because humans compete with it for recreation and living space on Florida's beaches. It spends the winter in South America, then returns to Florida each spring to nest on sandbars, beaches, and dunes. If it cannot find a suitable natural nesting site, it may lay its eggs on a gravel rooftop!

The Middle Beach

Tides are caused by the pull of the moon's gravity and the spinning of the earth. Two low tides and two high tides occur every day on Florida's Atlantic side. One to four tides of different heights occur on the Gulf side. Along Florida's Atlantic coast, the difference in water depth between high and low tides ranges from less than a meter (about 2 feet) near Miami to 2.5 meters (nearly 8 feet) near Jacksonville. The Gulf coast tides average less than a meter (only 2 to 3 feet) between high and low.

The middle beach is under water at high tide, but at low tide it is exposed to the hot Florida sun. Sometimes heavy rains bring fresh water into this salty environment, affecting the animals that live here.

Here, you may see birds running up and down the beach, dodging the waves. Or clams may close up their shells to keep moisture in when the tide is out, while crabs may burrow in the sand to keep from being washed away when the tide is changing.

Hermit Crab

Some animal shells grow larger and larger as the animal grows. Others outgrow the hard shell, discard it, and build a new, bigger one. Most crabs have hard shells, but the hermit crab has a soft body. To protect itself, it hides in the empty shells of snails. When it grows too big for its borrowed house, it crawls out and finds a larger shell to live in.

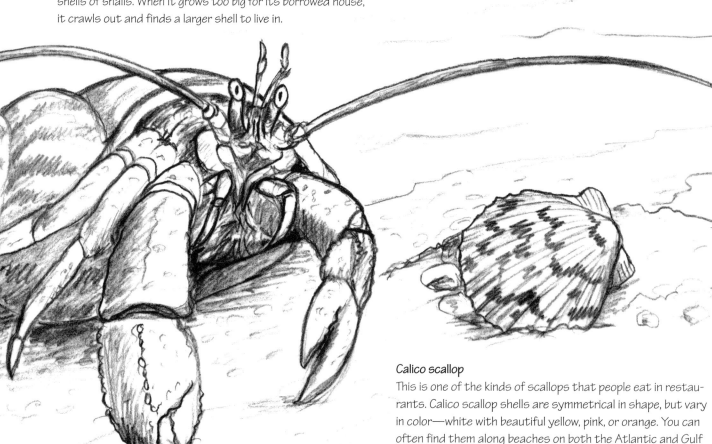

Calico scallop

This is one of the kinds of scallops that people eat in restaurants. Calico scallop shells are symmetrical in shape, but vary in color—white with beautiful yellow, pink, or orange. You can often find them along beaches on both the Atlantic and Gulf coasts.

Long-legged shorebirds

Sandpipers, willets, and lesser yellowlegs that run along the beach are all much smaller and plainer than the herons and egrets that are sometimes seen on the beach. Some shorebirds stay all year, some come for the winter, and others only pass through on migration. They wade near the edge of the surf in mixed flocks, searching for their favorite foods—marine insects, shellfish, or tiny crabs. Different shorebirds have bills and legs of different lengths, so they search for different kinds of food on different parts of the beach.

Wave-chasers

Sanderlings are the most numerous and familiar of the small birds at the beach. Flocks of sanderlings chase up and back as the waves flow in and out, running and turning together as though performing a dance, and picking at the coquina shellfish that are uncovered as the water goes out.

yellowlegs

willet

sandpiper

sanderlings

Coquina

The tiny coquina clam (not much bigger than your thumbnail) buries itself very rapidly as the waves recede. If you're watching closely, you can see a little squirt of water and the tiny dimple in the sand as it pulls itself down. You have to dig very fast to uncover it.

Their shells are pastel shades of pink and lavender. You can find many of them along the beach, often single shells, but sometimes two shells still attached in a pair and opened up like a butterfly. Coquina shells were used hundreds of years ago by the European settlers in Florida to make a rock-hard building material for houses and for the fort at St. Augustine.

Lettered olive

Smooth, glossy olive shells can be found washed up on Florida beaches. Lettered olives burrow deep in the sand and live together in colonies. They feed on dead crabs and clams.

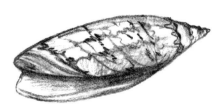

migration moving from one place to another with the seasons.

The Upper Beach

The upper beach is the area where the highest tides have reached, leaving a line of debris called sea wrack that drifts in from the ocean. Insects live in the decaying seaweed, and other animals forage for the insects. The sand is softer here, only occasionally packed hard by the waves.

Spooks!

Ghost crabs can be seen on the beach late in the evening. The ghost crab is ghostly white or sandy-colored and almost invisible as it scurries sideways across the sand. The ghost crab has gills that must stay wet in order for it to breathe, so it feeds on marine creatures in the cool of the night when the sun won't dry it out. It can live in the water or in the moist sand. When it outgrows its old shell, it crawls out and its body expands before its new, bigger shell hardens.

debris   an accumulation of plant, animal, or rock fragments.

sea wrack   debris from the ocean piled up in a row by wind and water.

Sargassum weed

The sargassum seaweed that grows and floats in huge mats in the Atlantic Ocean often breaks loose in rough seas and washes ashore. After a storm, you can find it along the beach in a long, brownish green drift line. If you turn over the seaweed and search among its leathery leaves, you will see the little brown balls filled with air that keep sargassum afloat. You might find other things, too—insects, crabs, or maybe a sea horse.

Sandfleas

Sometimes called sandhoppers, these little crustaceans burrow in the sand above the high tide mark, hopping about mostly at night and feeding on dead animal matter washed up by the waves. They are not insects and do not suck blood like the fleas on a dog, though they look something like a flea and can jump like one. They are also larger than a dog flea — 2 to 3 centimeters (up to an inch).

Oceangoing beans

Sometimes sea beans fall off vines and trees growing near the ocean in South America, Africa, and Australia and travel the world on the ocean waves. They can drift for many months and float as far as Florida. You may find some in the sea wrack washed up on the beach.

crustacean   a usually aquatic animal with an outside
   skeleton, such as lobsters and shrimp.
drift line   debris piled up in a row by wind and water;
   sea wrack.

The Dunes

Beyond the reach of the waves except during storms, the dunes rise in high mounds of soft, deep sand. Blown and piled up by the wind, dunes protect the plants and animals that live behind them from the salt spray, and provide a hot, desertlike habitat for an entirely different group of plants and animals.

Home from the sea

Loggerhead sea turtles lay their eggs on Florida's east coast beaches. Scientists know little about the turtles' lives in the deep ocean but are able to study them when the females come ashore in the summertime to lay their eggs. We do know that female sea turtles travel the seas for many miles and many years before they find their way back to the same beach where they were born to bury their eggs.

The adult loggerhead sea turtle can weigh over 150 kilograms (300 pounds), and its shell grows to over a meter (4 feet) long. Its large, blunt head gives it its name. The female comes ashore at night anytime from April to August, usually on a high tide. She leaves a broad track in the sand as she crawls to the upper beach near the edge of the dune. Her instinct tells her that she must make her nest above the high tide level so that her eggs are not washed away. Here, she digs a hole with her hind flippers and deposits up to 100 golf ball-sized eggs in it. Then she covers the hole and crawls back to the sea. Her heavy body and swimming flippers make her efforts on land difficult and slow. She may come ashore several times during the summer to lay more than one nest of eggs.

The sand, heated by the sun, keeps the eggs warm. Two to three months later, the baby turtles, small enough to fit in a tablespoon, hatch all together one night and dig their way up through the sand. They are attracted to the shine of moon and stars on the water and scramble for the safety of the waves. But if they are attracted by streetlights or hotel signs instead and do not find their way to the water, they may be eaten by raccoons or ghost crabs at night, or die from the hot sun or be eaten by gulls the next day.

Atlantic green turtles, hawksbills, and leatherbacks nest on Florida beaches, too, but only rarely and in much smaller numbers than the loggerhead.

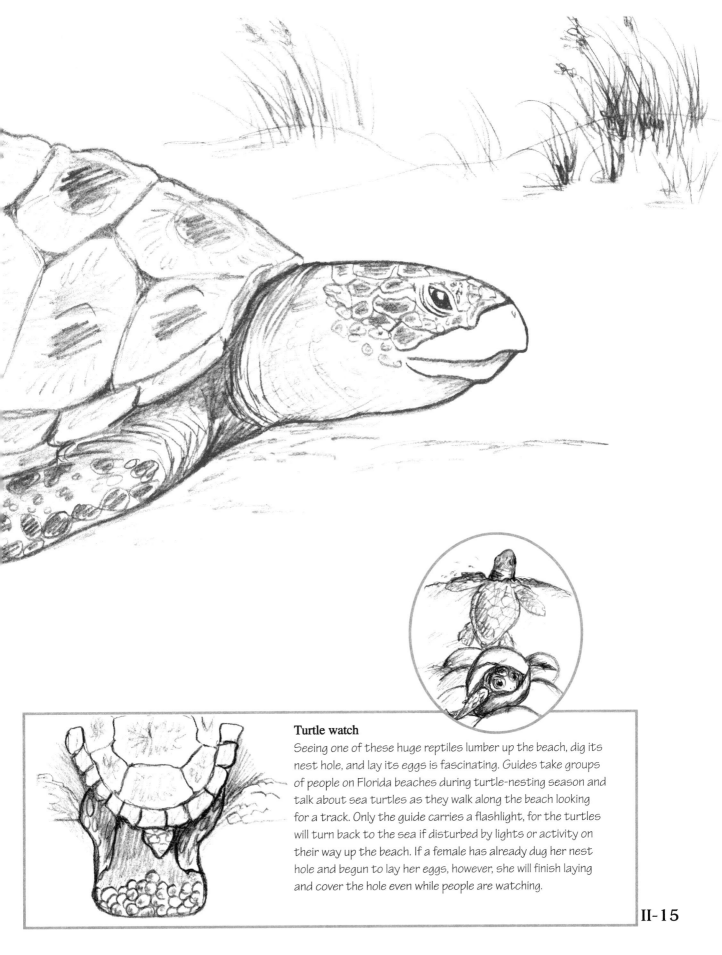

Turtle watch

Seeing one of these huge reptiles lumber up the beach, dig its nest hole, and lay its eggs is fascinating. Guides take groups of people on Florida beaches during turtle-nesting season and talk about sea turtles as they walk along the beach looking for a track. Only the guide carries a flashlight, for the turtles will turn back to the sea if disturbed by lights or activity on their way up the beach. If a female has already dug her nest hole and begun to lay her eggs, however, she will finish laying and cover the hole even while people are watching.

II-15

Plants of the Dunes

Plants that grow on the dunes of Florida must be able to survive salt spray, hot sun, and shifting sand. Occasionally plants will be washed over with salt water from storm waves.

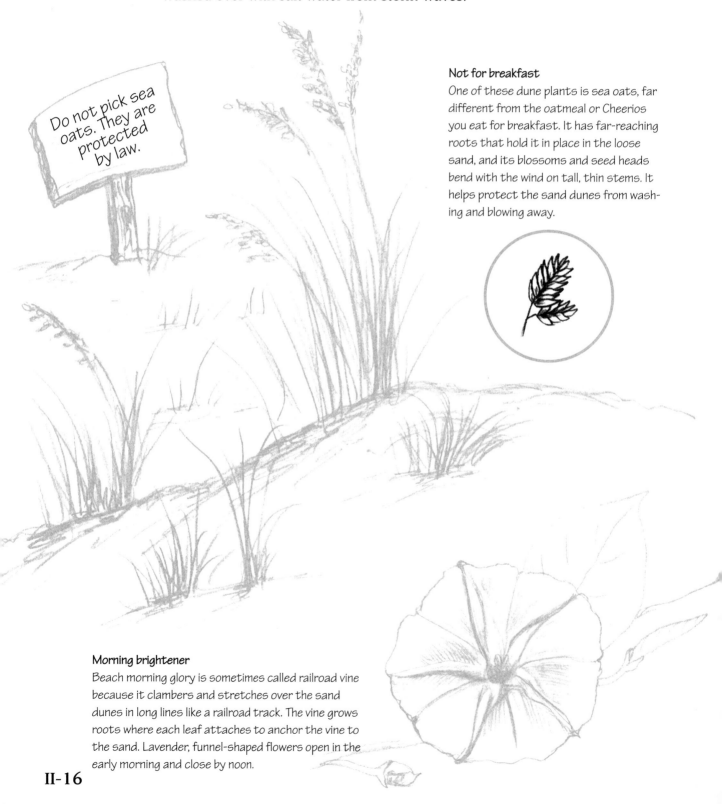

Do not pick sea oats. They are protected by law.

Not for breakfast

One of these dune plants is sea oats, far different from the oatmeal or Cheerios you eat for breakfast. It has far-reaching roots that hold it in place in the loose sand, and its blossoms and seed heads bend with the wind on tall, thin stems. It helps protect the sand dunes from washing and blowing away.

Morning brightener

Beach morning glory is sometimes called railroad vine because it clambers and stretches over the sand dunes in long lines like a railroad track. The vine grows roots where each leaf attaches to anchor the vine to the sand. Lavender, funnel-shaped flowers open in the early morning and close by noon.

prickly pear

sandspurs

saw palmetto

Spanish bayonet

Ouch!

Some of the plants that live on the dunes have sharp points on them. These prickly plants help protect small beach animals that hide among them from bigger animals that might eat them. They also help to keep people from walking over the dunes and disturbing the plants.

Sandspurs are grasses with clusters of pea-sized seeds that have short spikes all around them. If you step on one with a bare foot, it can stick painfully in your skin. The roots of these grassy plants help to hold the sand in place.

The prickly pear cactus has several finger-length thorns on each fleshy leaf pad.

Every leaf of the Spanish bayonet is a dangerous spear as long as your leg.

Saw palmettos grow thickly in many places in Florida, including beach dunes. Their broad leaves, called fronds, offer shade and shelter to small animals, but the stems of the fronds are saw-toothed. Most saw palmettos are shiny green, but in some areas the fronds are silvery or bluish.

Nice Mice

Beach mice live on barrier islands, separated from the mainland by lagoons. Beach mice are paler in color than mainland mice, perhaps to make it harder for hawks and foxes to see them against the sand. They live among the sea oats and saw palmettos and feed on the seeds. Most of the species of Florida beach mice are endangered.

Behind the Dunes

The habitat behind the dunes may be another dune, a strand of ocean scrub plants, a cabbage palm forest, a salt marsh of grasses and reeds, or a lagoon.

The plants that grow behind the dunes or on a second dune ridge are scrubby and stunted by salt spray. Their habitat is not quite as harsh as the beach and front dunes, but life here is not easy either. Small, straggly oak trees lean away from the constant sea-wind. Dwarf saw palmettos grow close together. Sometimes forests of cabbage palm trees with vines and beauty berry bushes cover the back dune.

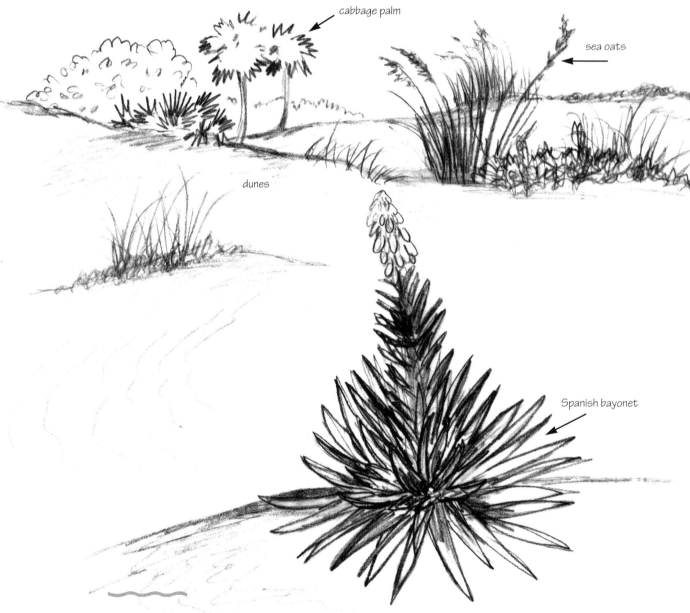

cabbage palm

sea oats

dunes

Spanish bayonet

lagoon a shallow water body partly surrounded by land that shelters it from the sea.

reed a tall, grasslike plant that grows in wet places.

strand a long, thin strip of land bordering a body of water.

Estuaries, Salt Marshes, and Lagoons

A barrier island may be separated from the mainland by an estuary, a salt marsh, or a lagoon. A long stretch of salt marshes also extends along the "bend" of Florida's Gulf coast, where there are no barrier islands. All of these habitats are places where salt water from the sea and fresh water from rivers and streams come together. The water in a lagoon or estuary is less salty than the sea and more salty than the fresh water running off the land.

Detritus washed off the land and plankton from the sea mix together in these watery places to form a soup that is rich in nutrients. This soup feeds microscopic animals, insects, and fish, which, in turn, are food for larger fish, birds, and mammals. Estuaries, salt marshes, and lagoons are very important in this cycle of life called the food chain.

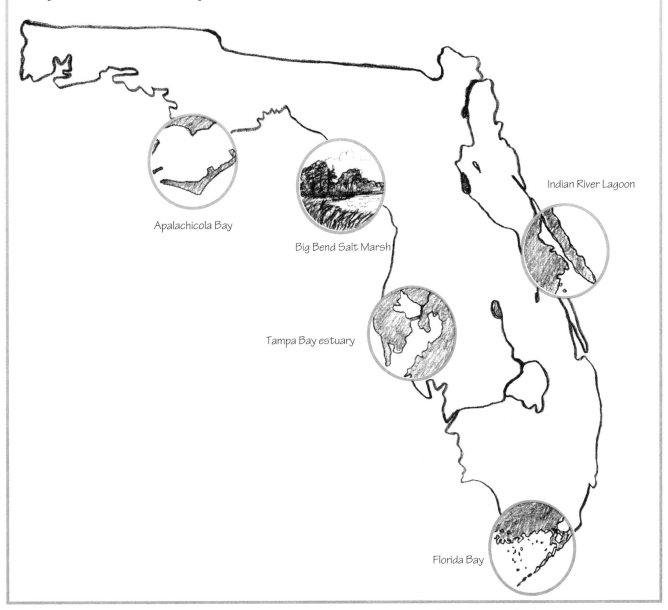

Apalachicola Bay

Big Bend Salt Marsh

Indian River Lagoon

Tampa Bay estuary

Florida Bay

detritus   particles of decayed animals and plants.
estuary   the watery area where a river meets the sea, where river flow meets the tide, and where fresh water meets salt water
food chain   the passage of food energy from plants, which make their own food from the energy of the sun, to animals that eat plants, to animals that eat other animals.

microscopic   too small to be seen without a magnifying lens.
nutrients   foods that promote growth.
plankton   microscopic plants and animals that drift in the sea.

Estuaries

Estuaries are places where a river meets the sea. The river current flowing outward meets the incoming tide to make a constantly changing mixture of saltiness. Some scientists think that estuaries are the most productive places in the world, where the young of many species hatch and grow, and where many species of crabs, oysters, and clams live out their lives.

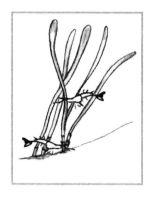

Underwater grassy meadows

Though the long, thin blades of sea grasses make them look like an overgrown lawn, they are not real grasses at all. They are a kind of plant—in fact, the only plant—that flowers and produces fruits and seeds in seawater. Florida's shallow estuaries have some of the biggest seagrass beds in the world. Most of the sea grasses grow in Florida Bay and near the coral reefs. The several species of sea grasses that occur in Florida provide food and shelter to most species of fish and shellfish during some part of their lives.

The journey of the pink shrimp

The female pink shrimp lays her eggs in deep ocean waters near south Florida. When the larvae hatch, they begin swimming and floating with the currents. They feed at night on plankton, shedding their shells as they outgrow them. About a month later, the young shrimp enter one of the shallow, grassy estuaries along the southwest coast of Florida. Here they feed on organisims on the seagrass blades and in the mud, growing to about 5 centimeters (2 inches) long in about two months. Then most of them leave the estuary, migrating back to the ocean on the falling tides. Those that are not eaten by snook and other fish, or are not netted by shrimp fishermen, may reach deep water again, growing bigger all the time. If they escape the commercial shrimp trawlers offshore, they continue to grow to as long as 18 centimeters (6 inches). In the spring, the females lay their eggs again in the waters off south Florida.

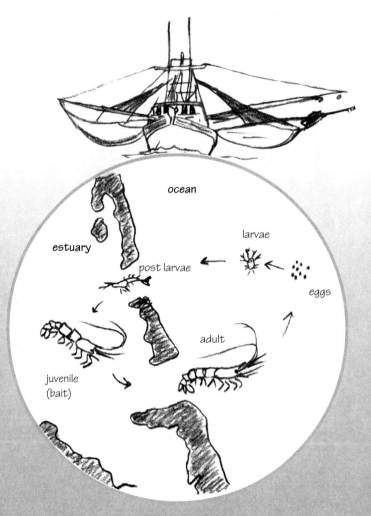

ocean

larvae

estuary

post larvae

eggs

adult

juvenile (bait)

larvae   the immature forms of an animal that are very different from the adult forms.

Blue crab

The blue crab lays its eggs in the sea far from the barrier islands. When the crab larvae hatch from the eggs, they float into the marshes and estuaries with the tides and feed on detritus in the muddy and sandy bottoms. A new generation of crabs then returns to the sea to lay eggs. Fishermen capture blue crabs for people to eat in special baited boxes.

Horseshoe crab

Horseshoe crabs live their lives in the ocean, then return to the estuaries and marshes on moonlit nights to mate and lay their eggs in the sand. These strange animals, with long, spiked tails and horseshoe-shaped shells, have ancient ancestors. Similar-looking fossils date back hundreds of millions of years. Horseshoe crabs are not true crabs. Their closest relatives are spiders and scorpions!

Oysters

Oysters are special seafood treats for many people. They are bivalves, with two matching shells that can be closed tightly for safety. They eat by sucking in seawater and filtering out nutrients. Many of Florida's oysters live their lives in a huge estuary at the mouth of the Apalachicola River in the Panhandle.

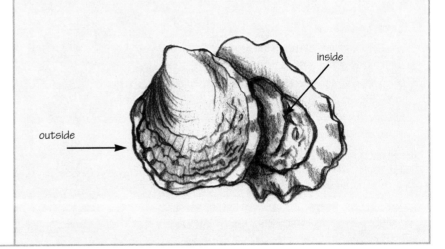

inside

outside

bivalve   an animal with two matching shells hinged together, such as a clam.

filtering   separating out particles from water.

fossil   a mineralized piece of a plant or animal from a past age. *Mineralized* means that, over a long time, hard nonliving material replaces soft living material.

Salt Marshes

Along some parts of Florida's flat coastline, the ocean tides flow inland over a large area, leaving the soil salty. The tides are shallow and the waves are small, leaving calm waters where certain sea grasses and animals can survive. These are the salt marshes.

Grasses called needlerush and cordgrass grow in some marshes. Leatherfern or sawgrass grow in others. A lone cabbage palm sometimes stands in the marsh.

Saltwater organisms that ride in on the tides find food and hiding places here. Insects, spiders, snails, crabs, and birds such as sparrows and wrens graze on the grasses or eat the algae and microscopic organisms in the marsh.

wren

sparrow

clapper rail

Little brown birds

Seaside sparrows and marsh wrens live nowhere else but in salt marshes. The sparrow's nest is lined with fine grass, and it often has a canopy over the top to hide it from predators and to protect the chicks from the sun. The seaside sparrow eats many different small creatures such as grasshoppers, snails, and spiders, as well as seeds. It has a buzzy call.

The marsh wren builds a coconut-shaped nest with an entrance in the side. The nest is made of grasses and cattails and lined with fine grasses, cattail fluff, and feathers. The marsh wren eats aquatic insects such as dragonflies and mosquito larvae, and its song is a bubbly trill.

Noisy bird

The clapper rail is a brownish, chickenlike bird that builds its nest in grasses or reeds in the salt marsh. It weaves the stalks into an overhead canopy so the nest cannot be easily seen from above. Eggs are laid in the spring, and the chicks leave the nest immediately after hatching. Although the rail is rarely seen, its clacking call can be heard in the marsh every few minutes most of the year. It feeds on crabs, snails, grasshoppers, and worms.

II-22   *organism*   a living plant or animal.

Creeks and rivers often run through the marshes, providing deeper water where fish and other ocean animals come in to lay eggs, hunt for food, or hide. Many offshore animals begin their lives in the salt marsh. Manatees live here. Land animals such as raccoons and skunks often come into the salt marsh to find food.

The Mosquito

The saltmarsh mosquito is one of the most annoying of all the 69 species of mosquitoes in Florida. It hatches in salt marshes and is blown by the wind or flies to inland places where the female bites people and animals. But the mosquito also is food for hundreds of species of fish and birds, in both its larval and adult stages.

The turtle

The diamondback terrapin is a turtle that lives in the salt waters of estuaries, salt marshes, and lagoons. It has special glands near its eyes to get rid of the salt, and a diamond-shaped pattern of growth rings on its shell.

The snake

The saltmarsh snake is related to Florida's other water snakes, but is the only Florida species that can live in salt water. It is not poisonous. It eats minnows and other small animals and is rarely seen during the day.

growth rings   layers that are produced in a single growing period in a tree or animal shell.

Lagoons

A shallow body of water between a large barrier island and the mainland may be called a lagoon, a bay, or a sound. It may be nearly enclosed by sandbars. Or it may run for miles—as does the Indian River lagoon—as a long inland waterway.

Lagoons provide protection for young aquatic animals because the water is often too shallow for larger fish that might eat them. The water inside a lagoon is calmer, too, buffered from the heavy wave action of the sea by a barrier island or sandbars.

The Indian River lagoon on the east coast of Florida runs for 260 kilometers (160 miles) from New Smyrna Beach to Jupiter Inlet.

Sea turtles, manatees, mullet, shrimp, horseshoe crabs, and many other animals rely on the special waters of lagoons for all or a part of their lives.

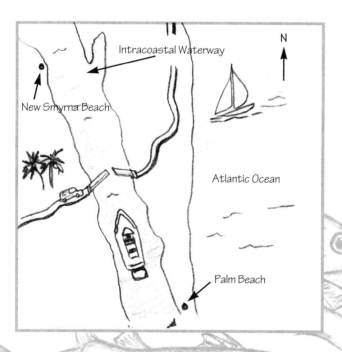

Intracoastal Waterway
Many of the lagoons, coastal rivers, tidal creeks, and marshes around Florida and along the Atlantic coast north of Florida have been connected by dredging a channel inside the barrier islands. This long waterway where boats can travel protected from the waves of the sea is called the Intracoastal Waterway.

A school of fish
Mullet run in large groups called schools in the salty waters of Florida's coast and move far inland up tidal creeks. They feed on algae and other tiny marine plants, and are, in turn, food for some of the large game fish such as tarpon, as well as for people. The fish you can see leaping high out of the water is often a mullet.

sound or **bay**   *a shallow body of water between a large barrier island and the mainland.*

The Mangrove Forest

Mangrove forests in Florida are found mainly on the state's southern coasts, for mangroves are trees that need warm weather and warm water.

Mangroves can live in salt water. They can live in fresh water, too, but they have more space if they grow in the salty, tide-washed areas of the coast because few other trees can grow there. Mangroves manage the salt in two different ways. The red mangrove filters out salt from the water at the surface of its roots. Black and white mangroves get rid of salt from the undersides of their leaves. Three species of mangroves grow in Florida.

Red

The red mangrove usually grows closest to the water's edge, where the tides wash in and out twice each day. When the tide comes in, thousands of red mangrove islands in Florida Bay are flooded, with no dry land anywhere under them. Birds can nest here in greater safety, because it is harder for predators to reach the forest through the high water. The red mangrove tree is easily recognized by its strange, stiltlike prop roots, which make it look as though it is walking on the water.

red mangrove

black mangrove

Black

The black mangrove usually is found growing inland of the red mangrove, on more sheltered, slightly higher ground. It can be recognized by the pencil-like air roots that stick up out of the mud below the trees. It withstands the chill of winter as far north as Cape Canaveral on the east coast and Cedar Key on the west coast.

White

The white mangrove grows even farther inland on higher ground where the action of waves and tides is small. It has no unusual root features, but it has two "bumps" near the base of each leaf that help it get rid of salt.

white mangrove

prop root   the curving support of a red mangrove tree.   **II-25**

Protector of Land and Animals

Mangrove forests are very important to the coastline of Florida. They help to hold shorelines in place during storms, preventing sand from washing away. They slow down floodwaters and reduce the destruction of heavy waves. They filter pollutants out of the water. They trap mud, leaves, and other debris among their prop roots and trunks. The leaves, flowers, insects, and other litter that fall from mangroves are an important part of the food chain, eaten by tiny, microscopic organisms, young fish and shrimp, and many other animals. The trees provide hiding places for small and young animals.

The mangrove forest is a nursery for young shrimp, spiny lobsters, snook, and snapper that feed and hide among the tree roots. Lizards, frogs, striped skunks, river otters, and the Everglades mink find a home in the mangrove forest. Fish swim among the prop roots of red mangroves, and oysters and sponges settle in the water beneath the trees.

The croc
The American crocodile is related to the alligator, but has a more pointed snout and greener color. It is endangered. Fewer than 400 live in the salt waters of the Florida Keys and the Everglades. American crocodiles feed mainly on fish and often swim in the mangrove creeks. The female crocodile builds a nest in the mud that is 1.5 meters (5 feet) to more than 7 meters (20 feet) across and half a meter (2 feet) or more high. She lays 20 to 80 eggs in the mound.

nursery   an area where the young of an animal lives during the early part of its life.

New trees from seeds

The seeds of mangroves begin to grow while still attached to the tree. A curved, pencil-like stem grows downward from the seed, 10 centimeters (a few inches) long on the white and black mangroves, but as much as 35 centimeters (a foot) long on the red mangrove. When the seed, with its stem, called a propagule, drops into the water, it floats in and out with the tides and the currents with the stem pointing down. If the tip touches a sand bar, tiny roots begin to grow out of it, anchoring the seed into the sand, and leaves then sprout from the top. Branches of the red mangrove grow out and turn downward toward the water, planting themselves in the sand to become the "prop roots" of a new tree.

Miniature violinist

The fiddler crab is small enough to curl up in a milk jug cap. The male crab has one large claw and one small claw. When he waves them around in the air, he looks like a bluegrass fiddler playing the violin. Fiddler crabs burrow by the hundreds in the wet sand in salt marshes and mangrove forests, especially among the pencil-like air roots of the black mangrove. They hide in their burrows during the day, out of the hot sun, but come creeping out in the early morning or late afternoon to feed on detritus, especially when the tide goes out.

propagule   a seed with its stem that begins to grow while still attached to the tree.

II-27

Dear little deer

The Key deer lives only in the Florida Keys, searching the mangrove swamps for food and hiding places. It is the size of a large dog—a miniature of the white-tailed deer that lives all over the eastern United States. It may be the only mammal that can safely drink salt water, for sources of fresh water on the Keys are few. The slender legs of the Key deer can scramble over the tangle of red mangrove prop roots amazingly fast. It is an endangered species, and has a national refuge to protect it.

Turtles and snakes

The mangrove diamondback terrapin and the mangrove saltmarsh snake live only in the mangrove forests of Florida Bay. They are only a little different from their saltmarsh cousins. This terrapin is different from other diamondback terrapins because it has raised bumps down the ridge of its shell.

The mangrove snake is usually dark with splotches on its back and light stripes along its neck. It is the only water snake that occurs in the mangroves.

Rosie

One of the most beautiful of Florida's mangrove-nesting birds is the roseate spoonbill. Its feathers are pink and bright red. Its broad, flattened, spoon-shaped bill is grayish brown, and it hunts for food by swishing its bill from side to side through the mud or shallow water. It builds its deep nest of sticks in the mangroves in Florida Bay and along the coast of south Florida, and may share its tree with the nests of ibis or herons.

Vireo

The black-whiskered vireo also nests in Florida's mangrove forests. It raises its family in the summertime and migrates to South America in the winter.

Cuckoo!

The mangrove cuckoo, as you can tell by its name, lives among the mangroves of Florida Bay and the Keys. It eats caterpillars and usually stays well hidden among the leaves.

II-29

Bird Hotels

Thousands of long-legged wading birds roost for the night and nest in colonies in mangrove forests. Sometimes the birds settle in such great flocks that the branches break. In the early 1900s, millions of birds nested in mangrove rookeries in south Florida, but human activities have reduced their numbers.

Most of these wading birds raise their young in the winter and spring dry season—December through May—when it is easier for them to catch the fish that crowd together in the shrinking ponds. They often fly far inland searching for food for their nestlings.

colonies   groups of the same kinds of animals living together.
rookeries   colonies of nesting birds.

The Value of Florida's Coastline

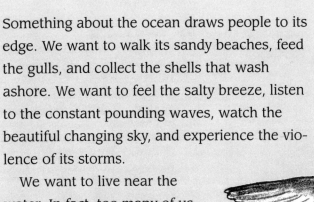

Something about the ocean draws people to its edge. We want to walk its sandy beaches, feed the gulls, and collect the shells that wash ashore. We want to feel the salty breeze, listen to the constant pounding waves, watch the beautiful changing sky, and experience the violence of its storms.

We want to live near the water. In fact, too many of us want to live near it, and much of Florida's coastline no longer provides a home to plants and animals that can live nowhere else—because we have cut down mangroves to see the water and filled in the salt marshes so we can build a house or get rid of the mosquitoes that hatch there.

We hope this book will help you care about the special places along Florida's long coastline and the plants and animals that live there.

barrier islands   narrow strips of land off the coast of Florida or other coastlines that run parallel to the coast.

bay   a shallow body of water between a large barrier island and the mainland.

bivalve   an animal with two matching shells hinged together, such as a clam.

buoy   a floating marker tied to the bottom to mark a channel or sandbar for boats.

colonies   groups of the same kinds of animals living together.

crustacean   an aquatic animal with an outside skeleton, such as lobsters and shrimp.

debris   an accumulation of plant, animal, or rock fragments.

detritus   (de-TRY-tus)   particles of decayed animals and plants.

drift line   debris piled up in a row by wind and water; sea wrack.

dune   a ridge of sand at the ocean's edge that is piled up by the wind.

ebb and flow   the falling (ebb) and rising (flow) of the tides.

estuary   the watery area where a river meets the sea, where river flow meets the tide, and where fresh water meets salt water.

filtering   separating out particles from water.

food chain   the passage of food energy from plants, which make their own food from the energy of the sun, to animals that eat plants, to animals that eat other animals.

fossil   a mineralized piece of a plant or animal from a past age. *Mineralized* means that, over a long time, hard nonliving material replaces soft living material.

growth rings   layers that are produced in a single growing period in a tree or animal shell.

habitat   a place where a plant or animal naturally grows and lives.

inlet   a narrow waterway opening of the coastline.

lagoon   a shallow water body partly surrounded by land that shelters it from the sea.

larvae   (LARV-eye)   the immature forms of an animal that are very different from the adult forms.

marine   in or about the sea.

microscopic   too small to be seen without a magnifying lens.

migration   moving from one place to another with the seasons.

nursery   an area where the young of an animal lives for the early part of its life.

nutrients   (NOO-tree-ints)   foods that promote growth.

offshore   out in the water a distance from the shore.

organism   a living plant or animal.

plankton   microscopic plants and animals that drift in the sea.

plumage   the entire covering of feathers on a bird.

prey   an animal that is eaten by another animal.

prop root   the curving support of a red mangrove tree.

propagule   a seed with its stem that begins to grow while still attached to the tree.

reed   a tall, grasslike plant that grows in wet places.

rookeries   colonies of nesting birds.

sandbar   a ridge of sand built up by currents in a body of water.

school   large number of fish of one species swimming together.

sea wrack   debris from the ocean piled up in a row by wind and water.

shellfish   an aquatic animal without a skeleton but with a shell.

sound   a shallow body of water between a large barrier island and the mainland.

species   (SPEE-sheez)   a kind of plant or animal.

storm surge   the increased height of the ocean along a coast caused by a hurricane.

strand   a long, thin strip of land bordering a body of water.

Coral Reefs

Under the blue-green water near the Florida Keys lies a magical world that few people see. It is a beautiful garden—a world of gorgeous colors, feathery plumes waving in the currents, creatures swimming, floating, crawling, or gliding everywhere you look.

These gardens are Florida's coral reefs, and they are places alive with activity—home to billions of tiny coral animals, schools of colorful fishes, graceful sea turtles, and other fascinating creatures.

But coral reefs are more than beautiful places admired by the snorkelers and scuba divers who swim here. Their solid, rocklike shapes form a barrier that protects Florida's coast from storm waves and provides boats with a safe place to anchor nearby. Fish and lobsters live in the reef's nooks and crannies, providing food for us and a livelihood for the people who catch them.

A mask and snorkel or a ride on a glass-bottomed boat are ways you can look down into this beautiful garden. This book will introduce you to some of the amazing creatures that live on the coral reefs of Florida.

What Is Coral?

Though some coral may look like boulders or feathery leaves, coral is neither a rock nor a plant, but a colony of living animals.

An individual coral animal is called a polyp. Each polyp is tiny—from the size of a pinhead to a thumbnail across, depending on the species.

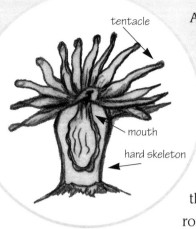

tentacle

mouth

hard skeleton

Although they are small, polyps are easily visible to snorkelers or swimmers with goggles. Coral polyps live inside a limestone cup they make themselves.

One end of a polyp's tube-like body is firmly attached to a hard surface. The opposite end is the animal's mouth, which is surrounded by a ring of tentacles that wave about in the ocean currents.

What's a Reef?

It's hard to believe that something as large as a coral reef could be built by tiny coral polyps no bigger than your fingernail! But each individual polyp helps the reef to grow by secreting a hard limestone cup around itself. When it grows large enough, it connects with the cups of nearby polyps, forming a continuous mat of living tissue—a reef. As the coral polyps crowd together, the reef grows larger and larger.

When coral polyps die, their soft body parts decay, but the hardened cups are left behind. New polyps then build their cups on top of the dead cups.

Coral reefs grow very slowly. It has taken thousands of years to build the reefs found in Florida.

---

colony   a group of the same kind of animal living together.
polyp   a marine animal with a tubelike body which is attached at one end to a hard surface and which has a mouth at the other end.

secrete   to release a substance.
species   a kind of plant or animal.
tentacles   a ring of food-gathering appendages surrounding the mouth of some marine animals.

Kinds of Reefs

Different kinds of coral grow in all the oceans of the world, but polyps need special environmental conditions to grow into huge reefs like those in Florida. Animals other than coral polyps can form reefs, too, and so can things that don't live naturally in the ocean (like shipwrecks and old tires).

Coral reefs

Coral polyps can grow into different reef shapes. In Florida, the most common are patch and bank reefs. Patch reefs are small "patches" of coral, usually surrounded by sea grasses. Near the Florida Keys, bank reefs grow parallel to the coast. Here, large growths of coral are separated by "valleys" of sand and coral rubble. Water currents pass through these valleys, bringing food to the coral polyps, and fish and other animals use the valleys as underwater "highways."

Worm reefs

A different kind of reef, called a worm reef, grows off the east coast of central Florida. These reefs are made by tropical marine worms instead of coral polyps.

Like the coral reefs, worm reefs also grow in shallow water not far from the coast. They are made up of tubes of sand grains cemented together by a gluelike material produced by the worm. The reefs grow larger as the larvae of the worms settle onto the existing masses of tubes.

Artificial reefs

Artificial reefs are made up of materials that are put in the sea by people, either by accident or on purpose. Shipwrecks and wrecked airplanes, bridge pilings and fishing piers, pipelines and navigation markers are all examples of artificial reefs.

Many of these large structures dumped in the sea haven't moved for many years, and communities of reef creatures have grown on and around the pieces of metal, wood, or concrete. Artificial reefs create places for algae, sponges, and corals to attach to, while animals that move, such as spiny lobsters, stone crabs, and fish, live nearby.

---

algae   certain plants that usually live in water.
larva   the immature form of an animal that is very different from its adult form.

rubble   pieces of broken coral.

Where Does Coral Grow?

To grow into reefs, corals need clear, salty, warm water—almost as warm as your bath water. Because they don't like cold water, coral animals can live only in shallow, sunlit areas of tropical and subtropical oceans. The only place along the entire North American continent that meets these conditions is the Atlantic coast south of Miami. Here, the Florida reefs extend about 290 kilometers (180 miles) along the Florida Keys past Key West to the Dry Tortugas.

Reefs do not grow along Florida's Gulf coast because the water is cooler and less clear, but individual corals, sometimes called coral heads, can grow as far north as Cedar Key.

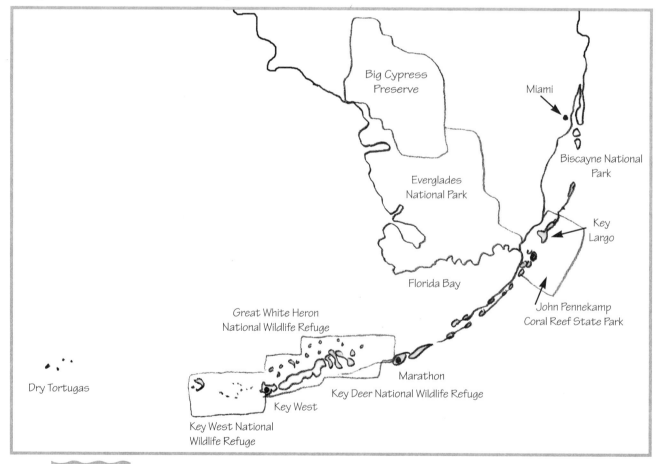

subtropical   situated in the region of the earth lying between the tropics and temperate lands (cooler than the tropics, warmer than the temperate areas).

tropical   situated in the tropics, a part of the earth's surface near the equator, where it is very warm.

How Does Coral Eat?

A polyp waves its tentacles outside its cuplike home, sweeping the water to catch food floating in the ocean currents. When food brushes the tentacles, special stinging cells called nematocysts stun the prey and capture it. Then the tentacles pull the food into the polyp's mouth. Coral animals feed upon plankton, floating organic materials, and even tiny fish.

How Does Coral Protect Itself?

Polyps feed at night, when—with masses of tentacles waving in the water—coral can look like a huge mound of fuzz! But during the daytime each polyp pulls its body almost completely inside its cup home, just like a turtle. This helps to keep it safe from grazing fish and other coral predators.

Another way a polyp protects itself is by oozing a slimy mucus that covers it and its neighbors. This mucus coating cleanses the polyps of silt and sand that could smother them.

---

graze   to feed on vegetation.
mucus   a slimy protective secretion.
nematocysts   stinging cells in tentacles of coral polyps, jellyfish, and anemones.
organic   made of living (or formerly living) plants or animals.

plankton   microscopic plants and animals that drift in the sea.
predator   an animal that hunts, kills, and eats other animals.
prey   an animal that is eaten by another animal.

Kinds of Coral

The many different species of coral that grow in Florida waters can be grouped into two kinds, depending on the type of cup they secrete—hard corals and soft corals.

Hard corals

The rocklike structures that eventually build up into a reef are the hard corals. Hard corals grow in many different sizes and shapes, and are often named for things they look like.

Staghorn coral

Staghorn coral is one of the major reef-building corals in Florida. It grows like a rack of antlers and forms clusters with pointed, brownish yellow tips.

Brain coral

There are several different kinds of brain coral, but in all species the polyps grow together in long rows separated by grooves that resemble the human brain.

Elkhorn coral

Elkhorn coral forms flat, golden branches that look like the wide antlers of an elk. It grows in shallow water, sometimes even sticking out of the water at low tide.

Sharp cups stick out on all the branches, and a diver or snorkeler must be very careful when swimming close to elkhorn coral to avoid getting cut.

Pillar coral

This coral grows in tall columns like a skyscraper or the spires of a cathedral. It looks fuzzy, because the polyps extend their feeding tentacles most of the time.

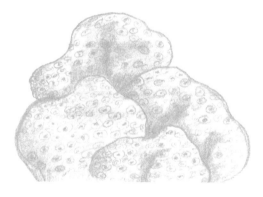

Boulder coral

Boulder coral has a pitted appearance, and it grows in different shapes. Sometimes it looks like a giant bean bag chair, or other times like a head of cabbage.

Soft corals

Soft corals make up a large part of Florida's underwater gardens. Their pleasing colors and gentle shapes, swaying in the current, look like plants growing on or near the reef, but they are coral animals all the same!

They are called soft because they don't create stony cups around their bodies like the hard corals. Instead, spicules—tiny, needlelike pieces of limestone in their tissue—support the polyp's soft body.

Like the hard corals, soft corals grow in different sizes and shapes.

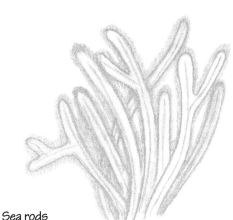

Sea rods
Sea rods are long, sticklike corals that sometimes grow so many branches, they look like underwater bushes.

Sea plumes
Sea plumes, or sea feathers, look like the soft feathers of an ostrich.

Sea fans
Sea fans form delicate, lacy patterns in the shape of a large fan, like the fans that ladies sometimes use to keep cool. They can be purple, yellow, or white.

Sea whips
Sea whips often grow in shallow water far away from the reef. They look like slender whips with their long, thin stalks attached to the hardbottom.

hardbottom   rocky areas of the sea floor.
spicules   internal skeletal elements of soft corals and sponges.

Coral, Coral, and More Coral!

Some corals can reproduce by releasing millions of microscopic eggs into the water. Some of the eggs ride the ocean currents for hundreds of miles before hatching. After a time, the free-living larvae that hatch from the eggs settle on the ocean floor and change into young coral polyps.

reproducing by eggs

In other species, a small piece of polyp may pinch off to form a new polyp through a process called "budding." These two polyps will produce two more, and those four will produce four more, and so on.

Sometimes coral can be broken during storms or rough seas. If the conditions are just right, these damaged pieces can firmly attach themselves to the sea bottom and grow to become new corals.

budding

Safe circle

Around many patch reefs and large coral heads is a circle of bare white sand called a halo. Grazing fish and sea urchins keep this area clear by feeding on the plant and animal life that lives around the coral. Because this open area can easily be seen by predators, fish venture into it only as far as they feel they can safely go with time for a quick dash back to the reef.

budding developing into a new individual from an outgrowth of the parent.

halo a ring of white sand surrounding certain corals, caused by grazing marine animals.

Zooxanthellae (say "zoe-uh-zan-THEL-lee")

Each coral polyp shares its home with tiny plants. The plants are a kind of algae called zooxanthellae that live and grow in the tissues of all coral polyps. The name in Greek means "little yellow animal-plant," so they are yellow plants living in an animal.

Zooxanthellae are so dependent on coral that they usually cannot survive in the ocean on their own. They need the coral for food and protection. And likewise, coral polyps use zooxanthellae to make oxygen and food for them. So the algae and the polyp benefit from, and depend upon, each other. This partnership is called symbiosis.

Without zooxanthellae, corals would not have their bright colors. These colors come from the pigments of zooxanthellae rather than from the coral animal itself. In fact, without zooxanthellae, there might not be any coral reefs!

Underwater, the bright colors of a coral reef show all the colors of the rainbow. But seen from the surface of the clear water of the Florida Keys, all reefs look golden brown, and it is hard to tell how deep they are. If you're in a boat and you see brown, you may be about to run aground.

symbiosis   a close relationship between two unlike organisms that live together.

zooxanthellae   algae that live in the tissues of corals and other organisms.

III-9

Night vs. Day

A reef is like an apartment building, with hollow spaces in between the coral that provide rooms for fish, crabs, and many other animals. But these apartments have two sets of "homeowners."

Some animals feed during the day—either on the reef or in nearby seagrass meadows—and come in at night to rest and sleep in the safety of the reef. Others rest in the reef during the day and take their turn to go out and feed at night.

Day

Night

Reef Creatures

Sponges

Sponges are everywhere on the reef, living on, under, and even between the corals. A sponge doesn't move about in order to find food, but is a sessile animal that attaches itself to the reef or hardbottom and lets food come to it. Sponges come in a variety of shapes and colors.

Loggerhead sponge

The loggerhead sponge is the largest species of sponge in Florida waters. Its tall, round shape looks like a big barrel or clothes basket. The holes and tunnels inside the sponge provide a safe home for many animals, and sometimes a thousand tiny shrimp live inside a single loggerhead sponge!

Sea anemones

Sea anemones are some of the most beautiful and colorful reef creatures. Like sponges, they can be found growing everywhere on the reef. They are related to the coral polyp, but compared to a tiny polyp, the fist-sized sea anemone is a giant!

Like a sponge, an anemone is a sessile animal, which means that it must grow attached to a hardbottom instead of sand or mud. An anemone will often stick out from a crack or crevice in the reef, its tentacles gently waving to and fro with the currents. But if something frightens it, the anemone will quickly pull its tentacles close to its body.

The tentacles are armed with stinging cells that can kill larger animals that touch them. However, some anemones provide shelter and protection for "guests" that live with the anemone but aren't harmed by its dangerous tentacles.

sessile   referring to animals that require something to attach to.

Cleaning shrimp

Cleaning shrimp, so called because they clean parasites off the skin of other animals, often wait at the tip of an anemone's tentacles for a fish to pass by.

One of the cleaning shrimp, the banded coral shrimp, is sometimes called the barber pole shrimp because of its pretty red and white stripes. As it hides among an anemone's tentacles, the shrimp waves its white antennae as a signal to advertise its special cleaning service. A reef fish that is infected with skin-irritating worms or parasites will see this advertising sign and ask for help by using special signals.

The coral shrimp recognizes that the fish is not an enemy, and moves onto the skin of the infected fish to pick away at these irritants. Sometimes several fish will line up at this cleaning station, waiting for their turn to be serviced!

parasite   an organism that lives in or on another
          organism, usually causing it harm.

Boring Creatures

Some plants and animals bore holes in the reef, creating ledges, cracks, caves, and tunnels. Creatures that bore holes include certain algae, clams, sponges, and worms.

Even though the actions of these plants and animals damage parts of the reef, the holes they create provide homes for other animals as well as for themselves. Crabs, clams, and worms live in the small holes. Fish and lobsters often hide in the larger, deeper holes near the bottom of the reef.

Christmas tree worm

The Christmas tree worm builds its tube home by boring into live coral. It has a crown of brightly colored tentacles that spreads out in the water to trap plankton. This crown looks just like a miniature Christmas tree. If the worm is disturbed, it snaps back into its tube.

Flamingo tongue snail

Covered with orange and black spots, the flamingo tongue snail feeds on the polyps of sea fans, sticking its tongue into the coral cups and sucking out the living tissue.

Red boring sponge

Most of the boring sponges break down dead coral, but some feed on living coral tissue. The red boring sponge creates holes in the reef by oozing an acid that eats away at dead coral skeletons.

Reef Protection

Every animal on the reef has its own special habitat, feeding area, and way of traveling. Some species move between the shallow waters close to the land and the deep waters far offshore. Others live all their lives near a specific type of coral, their bodies designed for feeding only in the narrow cracks and holes of a reef. Many animals also have special ways to protect themselves in their reef homes.

Safety in numbers

Some fish swim alone, seldom leaving the safety of the reef. Others swim together in a large group called a school.

Small fish such as grunts and tangs hover in schools above the reef. An attacking barracuda or grouper finds it very difficult to capture just one fish from such a large crowd. This reduces the chance that any individual fish will be eaten.

Hawksbill sea turtle

The hawksbill sea turtle, named for its hawklike beak, swims in the shallow waters near Florida's coral reefs, where it searches for sponges to eat. The beautiful shell of this turtle has been used to make tortoise-shell jewelry in the past, but now the turtle is protected.

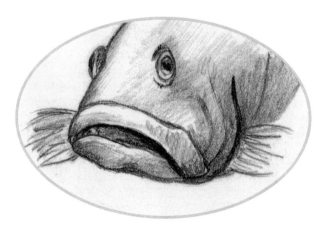

Color

The bright colors of some tropical fish help draw attention to their role in the reef community. In this silent, watery world, color can communicate to others of the same species to stay together in a school. Bright colors can also be a warning to other fish to stay away.

Some species change color as they grow; in others, male and female fish display different colors. Color also helps certain fish blend in with the different backgrounds of the reef.

habitat   *the place where a plant or animal naturally grows and lives.*

Patterns

Some fish, such as snapper and drum, are hard to see against the reef because spots, stripes, bars, or splotches help to break up the outline of the fish. These unusual patterns may hide important parts of a fish's body.

The four-eye butterflyfish displays two large spots near its tail that look just like eyes. But its real eyes are hidden in a band of black on its head. A predator aims for the false eyes, but misses its chance for a meal when the butterflyfish escapes in the opposite direction.

Now you see me, now you don't

Camouflage color helps protect animals from predators. They blend in with their surroundings, making it difficult for an enemy to see them.

The reef octopus is most often seen crawling along the bottom, searching for crabs to eat while it moves from one hiding place to another. It can change color instantly from red to gray to black to match the background. It can also discharge a jet of black ink to confuse its enemy while it makes a quick escape.

Reef Fish

More than 150 species of tropical fish live in and around Florida's coral reefs. Some of Florida's interesting reef fish include:

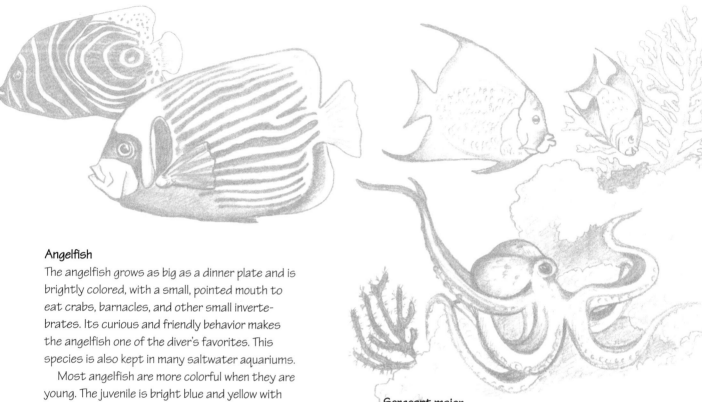

Angelfish

The angelfish grows as big as a dinner plate and is brightly colored, with a small, pointed mouth to eat crabs, barnacles, and other small invertebrates. Its curious and friendly behavior makes the angelfish one of the diver's favorites. This species is also kept in many saltwater aquariums.

Most angelfish are more colorful when they are young. The juvenile is bright blue and yellow with spots, but loses the spots and becomes an olive-brown color when it grows up.

Sergeant major

The sergeant major is probably the most common reef fish in Florida. Named for its militarylike stripes, it usually swims in schools above the reef, where it feeds on plankton. It darts into the shelter of the reef whenever it feels threatened.

invertebrate any animal without a backbone.

Butterflyfish

Butterflyfish are like teacup saucers in size and shape. They often travel in pairs. Each fish has a long "beak" that it pries into the cracks and crevices of corals and sponges to snap up little crabs and worms.

Grunts

Grunts swim in schools and are named for the sound they make. A grunt grinds its teeth together and amplifies the sound with a drumlike swim bladder, producing a groaning noise. A school of grunts croaking underwater can sound very strange indeed!

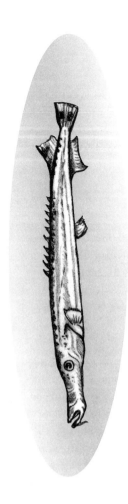

Trumpetfish

The slender trumpetfish hides by floating head down amid the soft sea whips and rods. A small fish swimming by might vanish instantly, inhaled by the lightning-fast gulp of the sneaky trumpetfish.

Squirrelfish

The large eyes and red-orange color of the squirrelfish make it very obvious in bright sunlight. But the squirrelfish lives in the dark tunnels of reef caverns by day, and there its red color appears black, making it hard to see. The squirrelfish comes out into the open water at night, when many other brightly colored reef fish are resting.

Parrotfish

Named for its "beak," which looks like a parrot's, a parrotfish uses its chisel-like teeth to grind large chunks of coral, trying to get at the polyps inside their cup homes. Once the polyps are digested, the skeletons—which by now have been ground into tiny particles—are passed out of the fish's body in a white cloud of sand.

Scientists think that a single parrotfish may crunch enough coral polyps to create more than a ton of sand each year!

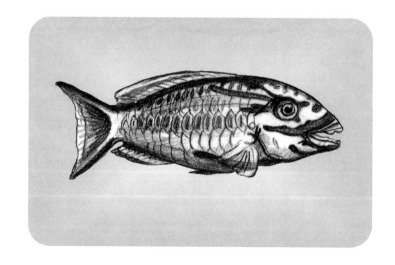

Wrasses

Some fish have colors that attract attention or advertise a special service, much like the cleaning shrimp. A colorful cleaning fish called a wrasse eats harmful parasites on the bodies of much larger fish, who might otherwise be expected to eat the minnow-sized wrasse. Predators recognize the bright colors of cleaners and do not harm them because of the useful service they perform.

Groupers

Huge groupers weighing up to 23 kilograms (50 pounds) lurk around caves and tunnels near the bottom of the reef. With a sudden burst of speed, a grouper can gulp a fish, crab, or lobster into its large mouth. Fishermen like to catch the different kinds of groupers because of their tasty flesh.

Reef Neighbors

Coral reefs can't exist by themselves. Like all ecosystems, they are linked to and depend upon other habitats farther away for food and energy. Many animals move between Florida's coral reefs and the mangrove forests and seagrass beds near shore or the deep water habitats far offshore.

Mangrove forests

Not far from the coral reefs, between the land of the Florida Keys and the shallow sea, are the mangrove forests. Three different kinds of mangrove trees grow here, and their roots help to trap the mangrove leaves and other plant detritus that fall or that wash in with the tides.

This leaf litter is broken down into tiny particles by microscopic animals and plants that feed upon the mangrove leaves. The particles are then dissolved in the sea water, where they provide food for filter-feeding sponges and barnacles and detritus feeders such as shrimp. In this way the mangrove forests are the bottom link in the food chain, helping to make food for the animals that live in the shallow waters around the reef.

Mangrove tree roots also provide shelter and hiding places for small fish and crabs. Larger fish move between the mangrove forests and the reef in search of food.

ecosystem   communities of plants and animals that naturally grow and live together.
detritus   particles of decayed animals and plants.

food chain   the passage of food energy from plants, which make their own food from the energy of the sun, to animals that eat plants, to animals that eat other animals.
microscopic   too small to be seen without a magnifying lens.

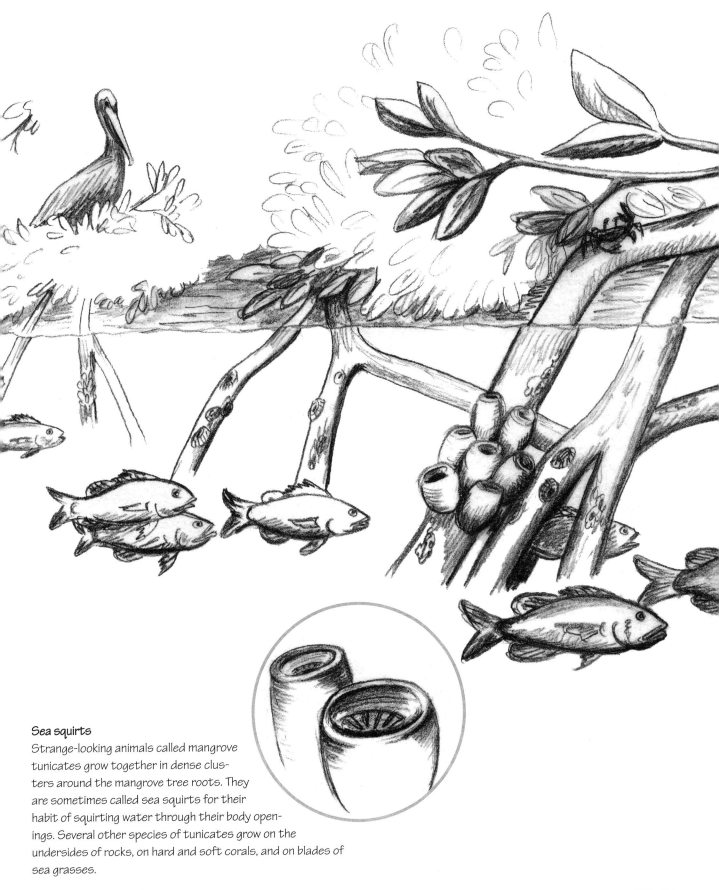

Sea squirts

Strange-looking animals called mangrove tunicates grow together in dense clusters around the mangrove tree roots. They are sometimes called sea squirts for their habit of squirting water through their body openings. Several other species of tunicates grow on the undersides of rocks, on hard and soft corals, and on blades of sea grasses.

Underwater meadows

Sea grasses are flowering plants that live in shallow seas, often close to coral reefs. They form vast underwater meadows that are important to the life cycles of many reef creatures.

Reef fish such as drums and sea bass hatch out and grow up in the seagrass meadows. They move to the reef as adults, but return to the sea grasses to lay their eggs.

Lobsters and snapper hide in the coral reefs during the day and feed in the seagrass meadows at night.

Sea grasses

Several species of sea grass occur in Florida, and three of them are very important. Turtle grass has large, ribbonlike blades (named because green sea turtles like to munch it). Shoal grass has very thin blades. Manatee grass has round, stringlike blades (guess who feeds on this!).

Seagrass blades provide a place to which organisms attach. The green algae that encrusts many grass blades is an example.

Don't call me a starfish!

Sea stars are benthic animals with prickly, spiny, or warty bodies. Some people call them starfish, even though they're not fish at all!

The cushion sea star is easy to see as it glides over the bottom of turtle grass beds. Its large, orange-red body looks like a seat cushion, and it uses its thick, stubby arms to search for snails on the surface of the sand.

Shaving brush algae

The common shaving brush is one of many kinds of algae. It looks like a man's old-fashioned shaving brush growing in the sandy soil near the reef. It has a short stalk topped by a whitish green, brushy head.

Tube worm

The shaggy parchment tube worm covers its paperlike tube home with pieces of shell, mangrove leaves, or pieces of turtle grass blades.

Upside-down jellyfish

The upside-down jellyfish is common in Florida. Sometimes hundreds of them cover the bottom where there is soft, mucky sediment and calm water.

It swims in a normal position for a jellyfish—that is, with its mouth downward—but it soon flops over, settling upside down in shallow water among the sea grasses. In this position, it soaks up the sunshine to turn it into food.

benthic   referring to animals that live on the bottom of the ocean.

Armed and Dangerous

Every animal that lives on the reef could become a meal for someone else. Camouflage coloration helps some reef creatures blend in with their environment, but other animals have developed unusual ways of protecting themselves.

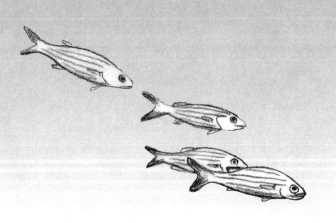

Fire coral

One of the most important corals for swimmers to recognize is fire coral, or stinging coral. If you touch it, it will feel as though you had stuck your finger in a fire, but after a few hours, the pain disappears.

The flat-topped fire coral is common in shallow water and also grows in large areas further offshore. It is easy to recognize with its mustard-yellow color and smooth, flat plates that are squared off at the top.

Moray eel

The spotted moray eel, as thick as a man's arm, slithers in and out of crevices in the reef. It sticks its long body out of a crack and opens a gaping mouth full of fanglike teeth to catch a fish swimming by.

Touch-me-not

Many sponges can cause irritation because of their rough skin. The fire sponge and touch-me-not sponge also contain poison that can cause a burning rash and swollen fingers if a person touches them.

Barracuda

The barracuda has a large mouth filled with razor-sharp teeth for capturing prey. It is streamlined for fast swimming and is one of the larger predators of the reef.

Though ferocious in appearance, it is not always a threat to swimmers or divers. The barracuda is unafraid and curious, and will often approach a diver and even follow one for a while. But even though it will not mistake a diver for a fish, treat the barracuda with respect.

Scorpionfish

The dark, spotted scorpionfish lies motionless on the ocean bottom, blending into the background so well that it is almost invisible. A row of poisonous spines grows beneath the eyes and along the fins to protect the scorpionfish from predators.

Bristles

The bristle worm is related to earthworms and leeches, and crawls about on coral feeding on the polyps. It has soft white patches along its body with needlelike bristles like a porcupine's quills that stick into the flesh of a predator. Also called the fire worm, the bristle worm can cause swimmers very painful wounds that sting for a long time.

Urchins

Sea urchins are slow-moving grazers that feed on blades of turtle grass or scrape algae off the surface of coral.

During the day the long-spined sea urchin hides in the reef under ledges, but at night it comes out to feed in the seagrass beds. Its needle-sharp spines repel predators and can pierce shoes and swim fins, causing painful puncture wounds.

III-26

The Spiny Lobster

Unlike the lobster found in cold waters, the Florida lobster doesn't have large pinching claws. Instead, to protect itself, the animal is covered with spines on its back and antennae and has a horn over each eye. The spiny lobster, sometimes called a crawfish, often sticks its long, brown-and-white, whiplike antennae out from under a ledge of coral. When it moves its antennae rapidly up and down, they produce a rattling noise that warns other lobsters to stay away.

A spiny lobster spends much of its adult life in the coral reef. But in its early life, it drifts in the water currents as a tiny larva in the zooplankton for several months before settling nearer the shore in the seagrass beds.

There the young lobster starts to grow and lives for a while, sometimes inside a loggerhead sponge or under a piece of coral rubble. It may travel between the sea grasses and the mangroves as it feeds, before moving farther offshore to live on a patch reef as a mature adult.

The spiny lobster hides in cracks and holes in the reef during the day, but returns to the seagrass beds at night to feed on small clams, crabs, or dead fish. In the autumn, adult spiny lobsters join together in a large group to travel in a long line—walking head to tail—out to deeper waters offshore.

The numbers of spiny lobsters have declined because too many people like to eat a lobster meal. Now, this species is protected in Florida waters.

The Queen of Conchs

The word conch (pronounced "konk") refers to a large group of snails that live throughout the world in shallow, clear seas and seagrass beds near coral reefs. Several species live in Florida, but the queen conch is the largest, nearly as big as a football when fully grown.

Like all other snails, the queen conch secretes a hard shell around itself that protects its soft body. The snail never leaves the shell, but does stretch its foot and head outside in order to move about and feed.

When frightened, the conch withdraws into the safety of its shell, using a horny claw on its foot as a door to keep out intruders.

The conch is a vegetarian that feeds upon algae and detritus by scraping food into its mouth with a hard strip on its tongue called a radula. Although a conch might look as though it's eating sea grass, it is actually feeding on the fine film of algae that grows on the seagrass blades.

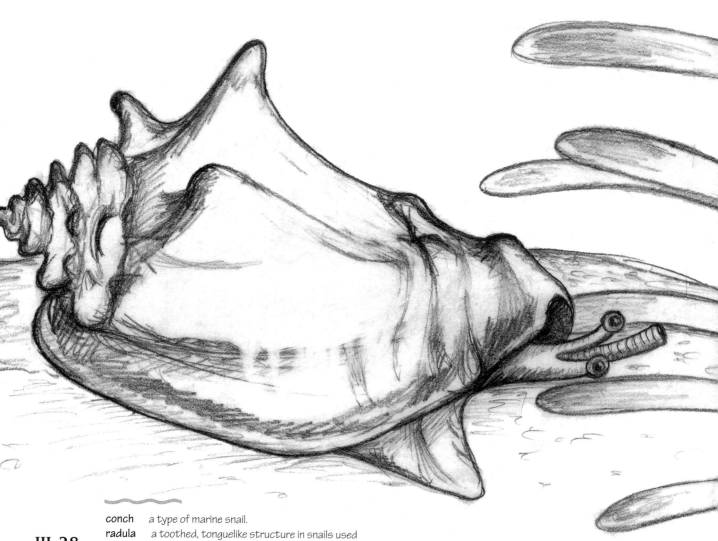

conch   a type of marine snail.
radula   a toothed, tonguelike structure in snails used
     for feeding.

In the summer the queen conch moves great distances to find food in the warm waters. But in the winter, when the shallow seas are rough and cold, the queen conch buries itself in the sand. Sometimes it rests with just the top of its shell sticking out. It may stay that way long enough to become covered with algae and sponges.

Conch is an important seafood, eaten by people as well as many animals, including hawksbill sea turtles, stingrays, spiny lobsters, hermit crabs, and octopuses. Early Native Americans used the conch shell to make tools and pottery. They also made it into a horn by chipping off the tip of the shell and blowing through it.

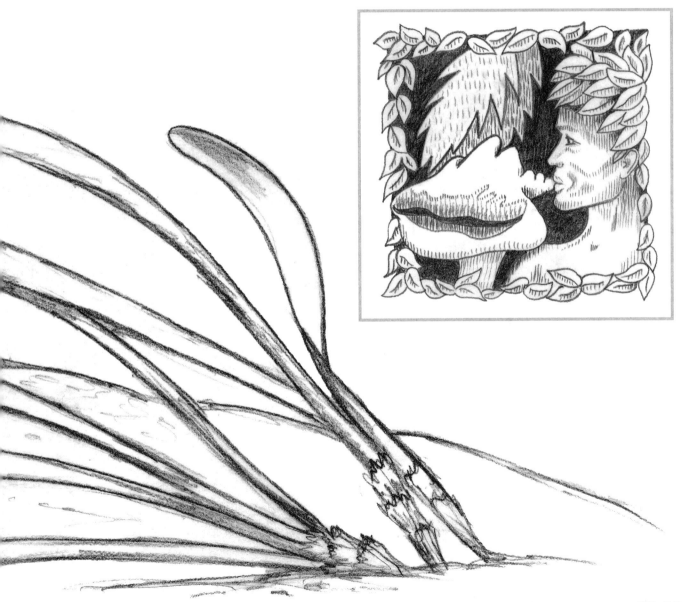

What Can Harm Florida's Reefs?

Even though it seems as though Florida's coral reefs are as strong as stone walls, able to take anything that nature can toss at them, many things—both natural and human-caused—can harm these fragile habitats.

Natural predators

Parrotfish can damage the coral when they break off chunks of it to feed on the polyps. Long-spined sea urchins graze upon the tiny plants and animals attached to the surface of coral. They also graze on coral larvae, preventing the growth of new polyps. Urchins can completely destroy the reef as they feed, leaving only coral skeletons behind.

Disease

Disease can injure and kill corals. One common coral disease is called black band disease. It is caused by bacteria that attack large species, such as boulder coral, when the coral's mucus covering has been damaged such as by parrotfish or a boat anchor. The bacteria then grow by feeding on the coral tissues, forming a dark band as they eat away at the coral.

Natural forces

Coral can dry out during very low tides, or high waves can wash some soft corals away. Many corals are choked by sand and sediment deposited on top of the reef by storm waves.

During winter cold spells, water temperatures around the reef drop, and the chilly water can harm reef animals, sometimes even killing them.

Coral bleaching

Water that is too warm can harm corals, as well as water that is too cold. Coral bleaching occurs when warm water temperatures cause the coral to lose their zooxanthellae. The corals lose their bright colors, and the coral polyps have little energy left for growth.

Why does this happen? Scientists are not sure, but it is known that an increase of only one or two degrees above the usual water temperature can be deadly.

bacteria   microscopic plantlike organisms, many of which cause disease.

sediment   material deposited by water, wind, or waves at the bottom of a body of water.

Conserving Florida's Endangered Reefs

Besides being damaged by nature, coral reefs are too often destroyed by things that humans do. In fact, the world's reefs are being damaged at a faster rate than they can grow back.

Florida's reefs are especially at risk because many people live close to them and many more travel to visit them each year. You can help save the reefs by knowing what causes them harm and doing your part to prevent reef damage.

Be a careful boater

Coral branches can easily be snagged by fishing nets, traps, and anchor lines, or broken by a boat's anchor, hull, or propeller.

Mooring buoys are floats carefully installed near some Florida reefs. Boaters can tie their boats to the buoys and never need to drop anchor on the reef. If you go for a boating trip with your family, always use a mooring buoy if one is available instead of the anchor.

Also when boating, never throw overboard tangled fishing line or other litter that can become trapped on the reef. Take it home with you to dispose of properly.

Swim responsibly

Snorkelers and scuba divers cause coral damage when they stand on or hold onto the coral. When you are swimming or snorkeling, remember that coral is a colony of tiny living animals and be careful not to touch it.

Take only pictures!

The beautiful colors of living coral reef animals soon fade when they are removed from their ocean home, so leave all creatures where you find them. Catch your animal with an underwater camera instead!

If we all do our best to protect the ocean environment, the beauty of these underwater gardens can be enjoyed by all who visit Florida's coral reefs.

Glossary

algae (AL-jee)   certain plants that usually live in water.

bacteria   microscopic plantlike organisms, many of which cause disease.

benthic   referring to animals that live on the bottom of the ocean.

budding   developing into a new individual from an outgrowth of the parent.

colony   a group of the same kind of animal living together.

conch (konk)   a type of marine snail.

detritus (de-TRY-tus)   particles of decayed animals and plants.

ecosystem (EE-ko-sis-tum)   communities of plants and animals that naturally grow and live together.

food chain   the passage of food energy from plants, which make their own food from the energy of the sun, to animals that eat plants, to animals that eat other animals.

graze   to feed on vegetation.

habitat   the place where a plant or animal naturally grows and lives.

halo   a ring of white sand surrounding certain corals caused by grazing marine animals.

hardbottom   rocky areas of the sea floor.

invertebrate   any animal without a backbone.

larva (plural: larvae [LARV-eye])   the immature form of an animal that is very different from its adult form.

microscopic   too small to be seen without a magnifying lens.

mucus   a slimy protective secretion.

nematocysts (nee-MAT-uh-sists)   stinging cells in tentacles of coral polyps, jellyfish, and anemones.

organic   made of living (or formerly living) plants or animals.

parasite   an organism that lives in or on another organism, usually causing it harm.

plankton   microscopic plants and animals that drift in the sea.

polyp (PAUL-lip)   a marine animal with a tubelike body which is attached at one end to a hard surface and which has a mouth at the other end.

predator   an animal that hunts, kills, and eats other animals.

prey   an animal that is eaten by another animal.

radula   a toothed, tonguelike structure in snails used for feeding.

rubble   pieces of broken coral.

secrete   to release a substance.

sediment   material deposited by water, wind, or waves at the bottom of a body of water.

sessile (SESS-ul)   referring to animals that require something to attach to.

species (SPEE-sheez)   a kind of plant or animal.

spicules   internal skeletal elements of soft corals and sponges.

subtropical   situated in the region of the earth lying between the tropics and temperate lands (cooler than the tropics, warmer than the temperate areas).

symbiosis   a close relationship between two unlike organisms that live together.

tentacles   a ring of food-gathering appendages surrounding the mouth of some marine animals.

tropical   situated in the tropics, a part of the earth's surface near the equator, where it is very warm.

zooplankton (ZOE-uh-plank-ton)   animal plankton.

zooxanthellae (zoe-uh-zan-THEL-lee)   algae that live in the tissues of corals and other organisms.

Oceans

When we stand on the top of a sand dune and look out across the ocean to the distant horizon, most of us see just the vast shining ripples and rolling waves breaking and foaming as they approach the shore. Unless a fin breaks the surface or a seabird dives in to catch a meal, we can only wonder about what's underneath.

It's not until we take a plunge beneath the waves, perhaps wearing a snorkel and mask or scuba tank, that we find the ocean is alive with a fantastic variety of creatures. In fact, every part of the ocean supports some kind of plant or animal life—no matter how warm or cold, or how deep and dark, the water might be.

The abundance of marine life found in Florida's offshore waters is truly astonishing. Imagine— over 1,000 species of saltwater fish have been identified here! And that number doesn't include the invertebrates, the animals without backbones, such as snails and jellyfish; nor the algae, grasses, and seaweeds; nor the masses of single-celled plants and animals called plankton; nor all the other creatures that call the ocean home.

This book will introduce you to some of the plants and animals that live in the water surrounding Florida's shores. So, come on! Take the plunge, and see the "Oceans Alive" for yourself!

Where Is Offshore?

Offshore means the open water—away from the sand, mud, or rocks of the beach, past the shallow seagrass beds and mangrove forests, beyond the barrier islands and coral reefs—far out to sea. Sometimes referred to as pelagic, this vast open area of the ocean is by far the largest of all the world's ecosystems.

Fewer plants and animals live in offshore waters than closer to the coast. Plants and animals need nutrients to live and grow. Nutrients include nitrates, phosphates, and other chemicals, and come from silt and organic materials in the soil.

Close to land, Florida rivers and lagoons pour nutrients into the ocean through inlets, where billions of gallons of fresh and brackish water move in and out with the tides. Pelagic waters receive few of these nutrients, for by the time they reach far offshore, they are diluted by the vast quantities of salty water in the open ocean.

brackish   slightly salty.
inlet   a narrow waterway opening of the coastline.
nutrients   foods that promote growth.
organic   made of living (or formerly living) plants or animals.

ecosystem   communities of plants and animals that naturally grow and live together.
pelagic   referring to the open sea.
silt   a fine layer of mud and clay.

Ocean Motion

Ocean waters are constantly in motion. Waves at the surface are caused by many forces—including the up and down movement of tides, the fall of rain, and even earthquakes—but primarily by the wind.

Currents below the surface are caused by wind, gravity, and differences in salinity and temperature. Some ocean currents transport warm or cold water over thousands of miles, affecting the climate of the land they pass by. Currents also transport fish, sea turtles, seaweeds, and ships.

River in the Sea

One of the strongest warm-water currents in the world flows around Florida. Near the Florida coast the Gulf Stream is known as the Florida Current. Like a huge river in the sea, this strong current carries warm water from the Gulf of Mexico around the tip of Florida. It hugs the ocean side of the Florida Keys, then travels northward into the Atlantic Ocean, staying close to the coast—sometimes just a few miles offshore—until it reaches offshore of Cape Canaveral. This jutting land mass directs the current farther eastward and into the open ocean.

evaporation   changing from a liquid to a vapor.
salinity   the amount of salt in the water.

Florida's Atlantic Side

The broad, sandy beaches along Florida's Atlantic coast gradually slope to the sea. As the land disappears under the water, it becomes the continental shelf. It declines until it reaches a rim where the shelf begins to slope steeply to the ocean floor.

Hardbottom

The sand or mud-covered ocean floor has rocky areas, called hardbottom. This provides a firm surface that animals, such as corals and sponges, attach to.

Many sedentary animals that can't move on their own live here. They depend upon the currents to bring them food and to remove their wastes. Animals that can move roam over the hardbottom and use the cracks and holes as hiding places.

Sea turtles come to feed on the sponges, lobsters, and conchs that live on the hardbottom, and they rest underneath the clifflike overhangs. Some fish are permanent residents, while others use these areas only seasonally. Hardbottom areas close to the edge of the Florida Current are often good places for fishermen to catch snapper, grouper, and sea bass.

continental shelf

ocean

ocean floor

continental shelf the sea bed surrounding a continent, the edge of which drops steeply to the ocean floor.

hardbottom rocky areas of the sea floor.
sedentary moving about very little.

A sponge is an animal

Sponges are simple animals that live on the hardbottom. Many sponges have glasslike skeletons that support a tough outer skin, giving them different shapes.

A sponge is a sessile animal, meaning it needs something—a shell, rock, or coral reef—to attach to. Instead of chasing food, it filters microscopic plants and animals through water canals in its body. It is porous—like a sponge!—with small pores, or holes, that let water and oxygen flow in. Larger pores allow wastes mixed in the seawater to flow out.

The sponge you use in your bath is probably synthetic, though people used to use real sponges. You can still buy bath sponges made from once-living animals, but they are quite expensive. If you should ever find a sponge on the beach or buy a real one in a store, remember this is the soft skeleton of an animal that once was firmly anchored to the sea floor.

Tube sponge

One of the sponges you can sometimes find while beachcombing is a tube sponge. It grows in a cluster of open-ended tubes and can be as long as your arm. It is pale blue when alive, but bleaches to a grayish white color when dead.

Red beard sponge

This colorful, orange-red sponge grows in beardlike strands on piers and pilings as well as on oyster-shell beds, shipwrecks, or hard-bottom in deeper water. Although this sponge is not harmful to people, other red or orange species sting, so avoid touching any brightly colored sponges.

microscopic   too small to be seen without a magnifying lens.
porous   having pores, or holes, through which water can flow.
sessile   referring to animals that require something to attach to.
species   a kind of plant or animal.
synthetic   not natural, but man-made by chemical processes.

Florida's Gulf Side

Sometimes called "America's Sea," the Gulf of Mexico covers some 1,500,000 kilometers (600,000 square miles), is over 3.2 kilometers (2 miles) deep, and borders Florida, four other states, and the country of Mexico. Along the west coast of Florida, the continental shelf extends in a broad, shallow expanse far out into the Gulf of Mexico.

Gulfside waters are often cloudy with silt and other particles, particularly near the mouths of large rivers where the incoming tide and outflowing river waters mix. Much of the Gulf bottom is mud and sand with few hardbottom communities, although storms and hurricanes sometimes expose more hard surfaces that animals and plants can colonize.

Living Seashells

Hard-shelled clam ⟶

Many species of clams inhabit offshore waters in the Gulf of Mexico. A clam uses a strong muscle, called a foot, to burrow deeply into the bottom. Clams are called bivalves because the soft parts of the clam are held inside two (bi-) hinged, hard shells, or valves.

Hard-shelled clams survive under difficult conditions. A clam larva must swim or crawl over the mud-covered bottom until it finds a suitable surface to attach to or burrow into.

Pen shell

The pen shell lives with its narrow end buried in soft, sandy mud. It spins a thread that helps it attach to loose stones or broken shells along the bottom. If it is uprooted by a predator or a storm, its thin, brittle shell soon breaks, and you may find the pieces washed up on a nearby beach.

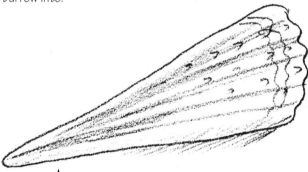

Perverse whelk

The perverse whelk is a snail that feeds on hard-shelled clams along the muddy bottoms of Florida's Gulf coast.

An adult whelk has a very heavy shell, often with spines near the top. If you hold most whelk species from the top, the hole is on the right. But the opening on the perverse whelk is on the left.

A female whelk lays a long string of egg capsules that look like little plastic pouches lined up in a row. One end of the string is cemented to a rock or dead shell, while the other end floats in the currents until the eggs hatch. As many as 100 tiny snails grow inside each pouch and soon escape into the sea through a hole near the top.

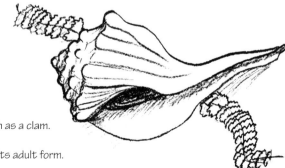

bivalve an animal with two matching shells hinged together, such as a clam.
colonize to settle as a group and grow in a new environment.
larva an immature form of an animal that is very different from its adult form.
predator an animal that hunts, kills, and eats other animals.

Dry Tortugas

Far out into the Gulf waters, more than 100 kilometers (70 miles) beyond the United States' southernmost city of Key West, lie seven small islands known as the Dry Tortugas. They were first named *Las Tortugas*—Spanish words meaning "the turtles"—because of the great numbers of sea turtles that used to be seen here. "Dry" was added later by sailors because no fresh water can be found on any of the islands.

The Dry Tortugas is now a national park and an important refuge for wildlife. It offers protection to a large colony of sooty terns, a species of seabird that nests here.

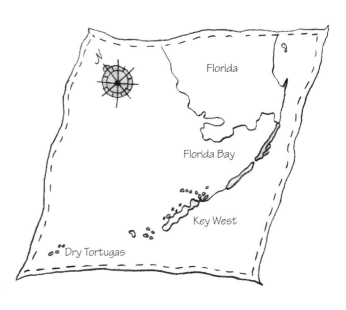

Sooties

Sooty terns are true pelagic birds that spend much of the year at sea. But during the nesting season they must find land. On Bush Key in the Dry Tortugas, more than 100,000 sooty terns nest closely together in a colony.

Called "wide-awakes" because of their nonstop calls, sooties busily raise their families from March, when eggs are laid, till September. Then the birds leave the island and fly thousands of miles across the open ocean to their winter home off the coast of Africa.

colony   *a group of the same kind of animal living together.*   **IV-7**

Drifters

Phytoplankton (say "FIE-toe-plank-tun")

Most land creatures have homes of some sort—nests, dens, or holes—but in the ocean, billions of animals swim or drift along their entire lives, going with the flow. Some live near the surface, close to the sunlight, while others move up and down through the water column in order to capture whatever food is available.

Food for many ocean creatures—from tiny shrimp to the biggest whale—includes a living soup made of tiny microscopic plants and animals called plankton. Plant plankton is called phytoplankton, and animal plankton is called zooplankton.

Diatoms

One of the most important food sources in the ocean is a yellow-green alga. Billions of phytoplankton called diatoms drift in offshore waters. They enclose themselves in glassy, shell-like structures with beautiful shapes and patterns.

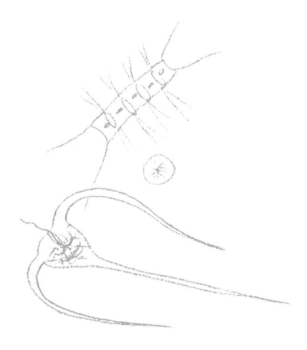

Dinoflagellates

Another important phytoplankton, called a dinoflagellate, looks like both a plant and an animal plankton. It swims instead of just drifting by propelling itself with a hairlike structure called a flagellum in grooves along its body. Diatoms and dinoflagellates are eaten by zooplankton and many larger creatures, such as oysters and clams.

---

alga   one of certain plants that usually live in water. The plural—algae—is used more often.
flagellum   a long, hairlike growth from a cell that helps it move.
phytoplankton   plant plankton.
plankton   microscopic plants and animals that drift in the sea.
water column   the space from the water surface to the ocean floor.
zooplankton   animal plankton.

Phytoplankton, a living soup

Phytoplankton is made up of tiny, usually single-celled plants. Phytoplankton uses the energy of the sun to make food, as all plants do.

The great mass of phytoplankton that drifts near the surface, closest to the sunlight, is the lowest line of the food chain. Animals that eat plants feed upon phytoplankton, and some of them are then eaten by other animals.

Plankton gone wild

Phytoplankton needs sunlight to grow, and it also needs certain essential nutrients in the water. But too many nutrients can create problems. During Florida's rainy season, fertilizers from farms and lawns and seepage from septic tanks run off the land into nearby waters, eventually reaching the deeper waters of the Gulf and the ocean. This can cause unusual growths of phytoplankton, called blooms, that prevent other marine plants and animals from receiving the sunlight and oxygen they need.

Red tide

Certain types of dinoflagellates cause occasional massive blooms, called red tide, that turns sea water a reddish brown color. Poisons produced by the dinoflagellates can kill fish and shellfish. Red tide can even cause the death of manatees and create breathing problems for people.

blooms   unusually high growths of phytoplankton.
food chain   the passage of food energy from plants, which make their own food from the energy of the sun, to animals that eat plants, to animals that eat other animals.

More Drifters

Zooplankton (say "ZOE-uh-plank-tun")

Zooplankton are animal plankton. During the day, zooplankton and other marine organisms move up the water column to feed upon phytoplankton found closer to the sunlight.

Some species of zooplankton are destined to stay plankton for their entire lives. They drift about in the open ocean feeding on other plankton and being eaten by fish, whales, crabs, and snails.

But other zooplankton are larvae and spend only part of their lives in this floating state. As they grow, they change. Leaving behind the characteristics of zooplankton, they eventually become adult worms, jellyfish, crabs, or barnacles, depending on their species.

Goose barnacles

A barnacle is a shrimplike animal encased within a shell made of hard, calcareous plates. A young barnacle begins life as a zooplankton, but soon settles onto a hard surface, such as a piling, a log, a drifting bottle, or even a sea turtle's back! Here it changes into a stalked, sessile animal protected by its hardened plates.

You can sometimes find goose barnacles attached to old boards, bottles, or other debris that washes up on the beach. Their name comes from an old myth that goose barnacles turned into geese, perhaps because the long stalk of the barnacle resembles a goose's neck.

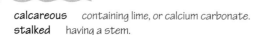

calcareous containing lime, or calcium carbonate.
stalked having a stem.

Glowing Waters

Sometimes at night ocean waters glow with a brilliant blue light that blinks on and off like a firefly. You can see it in a boat's wake on a dark night or when a big fish moves through the water. This glow, called bioluminescence, is produced by billions of plankton creatures.

Few bioluminescent creatures glow all night long, except when they want to attract prey or communicate. Most are invisible in the darkness until disturbed, when they turn on their special glow and light up the ocean.

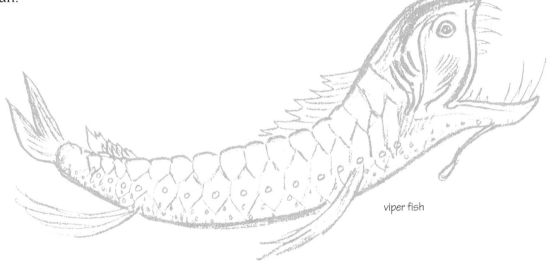

viper fish

angler fish

Fish that flash

Scientists believe that many deep-sea creatures are bioluminescent. The viper fish uses lights inside its mouth to lure prey into a trap. The angler fish wiggles a special lighted appendage—like a fishing pole—over its head to attract small fish who come to investigate and then become dinner. Other fish use their light to attract mates or to communicate with other members of their species.

appendage   an attached body part.
bioluminescence   light given off by living organisms.

Plants That Drift

Most marine plants are algae and are too small to be seen except under a microscope. But even those that are not microscopic are often difficult to identify because very few species of marine plants have flowers, roots, stems, or leaves as plants do on dry land.

Although few in number, marine plants are an important source of food and shelter to many other organisms.

Sargassum and fellow travelers

The golden-brown sargassum weed, or gulf weed, is a marine algae with berrylike floats that help it drift at sea. Huge masses of sargassum weed collect far off the Florida coast in a part of the Atlantic Ocean known as the Sargasso Sea. Sometimes you can find it washed ashore in large mats.

Some animals hitch a ride or find a home in floating seaweed drifting in the currents. Some camouflage themselves from attackers by taking on the color of the host plant. When storm winds or currents break loose clumps of sargassum, these clumps and their fellow travelers float along, making up a unique micro-community where several plants and animals live together in their own small world.

Sargassum crabs

These crabs live in mid-ocean, hitching a ride with sargassum weed in the Gulf Stream currents. In fact, the scientific name of one species means "little wanderer." Waving its tiny claws about the berrylike floats, it eats some of its fellow travelers.

micro-community   a small, specialized habitat of plants and animals.

Sea slugs

Nudibranchs, sometimes called sea slugs, are among the most beautiful marine creatures, in spite of their not-so-beautiful name. They are related to the more familiar snail or clam, though most nudibranchs do not have an external shell.

The sargassum nudibranch lives in sargassum weed. Its olive-brown body with specks of white, orange, and brown allows it to blend in with the golden stalks of its plant host.

nickernut

Sea beans

Seeds from marine and land plants drift in the ocean. Sea beans are the seeds of tropical vines and trees that fell from the parent plant on an island or in a rainforest and washed out to sea. They may drift with the Gulf Stream and other ocean currents for a long time before finally washing onto a beach thousands of miles away.

The sea bean most commonly found on Florida beaches is sometimes called the hamburger bean, because it has a dark stripe around the middle that appears to be held between two lighter-colored "buns."

hamburger bean

sea heart

Seaweed suppers

Marine plants are important to people, too. Many cultures use certain seaweeds every day in the foods they prepare. You might not know that you eat seaweed in ice cream and chocolate milk, and use it in toothpaste, cosmetics, and certain medicines. Other seaweeds are ground up and used for animal feed, fertilizers, and garden mulch.

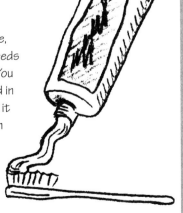

nudibranch   a sea slug whose name means "bare gills."

Animals That Drift

Even though water is their home, many animals that live in the ocean are not good swimmers. Like plankton and marine plants, many invertebrates depend on the waves and currents to move them about, although some can also move under their own power.

Invertebrates

Many of the animals that live in the ocean are invertebrates, meaning they have no backbone. Oysters, crabs, snails, and jellyfish are all invertebrates.

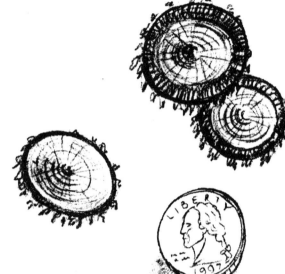

Blue buttons

Tiny, round, pale-blue discs called blue buttons float on the surface of tropical waters and sometimes wash up on Florida beaches by the thousands. About the size of a quarter, these harmless little jellyfish are fringed with delicate blue tentacles.

By-the-wind-sailor

Also called Velella, this tiny, violet-colored jellyfish has air chambers that allow it to float and a transparent triangular fin that extends above the suface, like a sail, to catch the wind and blow it along.

There's no shortage of these jellyfish in the sea. A ship reported sailing through and being surrounded by Velella for five solid days, as it travelled nearly 3700 kilometers (2,000 nautical miles)!

Swimming sea snails and sea slugs eat by-the-wind-sailors and blue buttons. By attacking and feeding on the tiny tentacles from underneath, they are unharmed by the stinging cells.

invertebrate   any animal without a backbone.
marine   in or about the sea.
nautical mile   a measurement used in ocean navigation, equal to 1852 meters (6076 feet).
tentacles   a ring of food-gathering appendages surrounding the mouth of some marine animals.

Neither jelly nor fish

A jellyfish floats gracefully through the sea with long tentacles trailing beneath it, or swims by opening and closing its body wall like an umbrella.

Jellyfish are not fish at all. They vary in size, shape, and color, but many look like plastic bags filled with a squishy, jellylike material.

Most jellyfish have stinging cells, called nematocysts, on tentacles that rim the mouth. Each nematocyst is like a miniature harpoon loaded with poison that can be shot out to catch plankton, small fish, or even other jellyfish. Each nematocyst is used only once, and a new stinging cell grows to take its place.

Cannonball jellyfish

Growing nearly to the size of a bowling ball (or cannonball, in the days when it was named) this brownish jellyfish is a strong swimmer. Under water, its jellylike material appears very thick and looks like half an egg—a very big egg!

Deadly balloons

Beachcombers in Florida often find the beautiful but dangerous Portuguese man-of-war jellyfish washed up on the beach, looking like a harmless purple balloon. If you step on one of them, the float makes a popping sound, but you will regret it. Touching the tentacles causes severe pain. Swimmers in the ocean should be on the lookout for the animal's long tentacles, armed with powerful stinging cells. Tentacles may trail out behind as much as 15 meters (50 feet)! Alive or dead, Portuguese-men-of-war always should be avoided.

Comb jelly cowboys

A comb jelly gets its name from the rows of fringed hairs, resembling tiny combs, that beat together to propel it through the water. Although it has no stinging nematocysts, a comb jelly can rope and kill other sea jellies and small fish using special sticky cells, called lasso cells, that latch onto the prey as it swims by.

Small, delicate, and beautiful to look at, a comb jelly catches the sunlight and refracts it, creating rainbow colors along its translucent body. Comb jellies are also bioluminescent and flash in the water at night.

nematocysts   stinging cells in the tentacles of coral polyps, jellyfish, and anemones.
refract   to change the direction of a light wave.
translucent   allowing light to partially pass through.

What eats a jellyfish?

Although it may seem hard to believe, the world's largest sea turtle lives on a diet of jellyfish! The leatherback sea turtle can dive to great depths—more than 300 meters (1,000 feet)—in search of jellyfish. Stiff spines in its throat project backwards to help the turtle swallow its soft prey.

Sea turtles sometimes mistake plastic in the ocean— sandwich bags or balloons floating on the surface—for soft-bodied animals such as the Portuguese-man-of-war. If a leatherback eats the plastic, it could die.

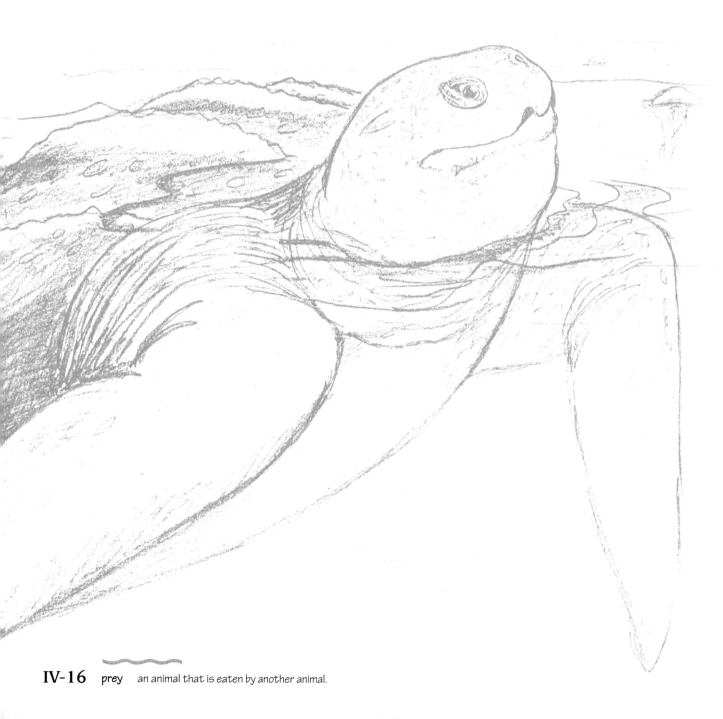

prey an animal that is eaten by another animal.

Swimmers

Some zooplankton, when they grow into adults, join the ranks of free-swimming creatures of the sea. Plankton move at the mercy of the currents, but the swimmers of the ocean are streamlined and move independently of ocean currents.

Fish facts

Most fish begin their lives as tiny eggs adrift in the sea. Larvae develop inside the eggs, and when they hatch they feed on plankton until they develop into young fish.

Fish are cold-blooded animals that breathe through gills and have fins instead of arms and legs. They are vertebrates, and most fish have skeletons made of bone. A few, such as sharks, rays, and skates, have cartilage instead of bone. We have cartilage in our bodies, too—push gently on your ear or the end of your nose to feel it!

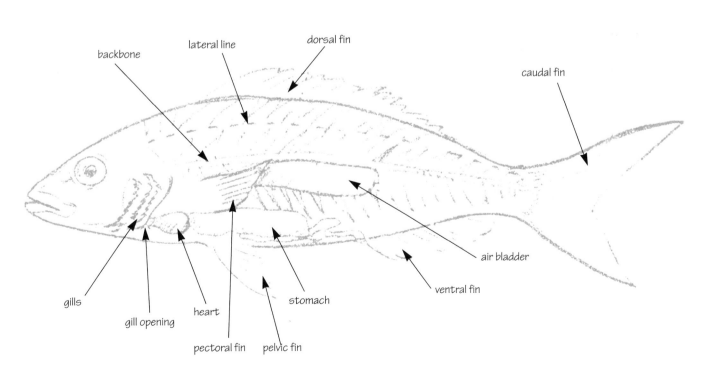

cartilage   semi-hard, elastic-like tissue that takes the place of a skeleton in some animals.
vertebrate   an animal with a backbone.

Fish Features

Survival is the name of the game for all animals, including those that live in the sea.
Many fish have unique—even bizarre—ways to survive.

Barbels

Barbels may look like whiskers, but they are feelers that help a fish find and taste food. The black drum has 10 to 14 pairs of tiny barbels on its chin. The sea catfish has 4-6 long barbels around its mouth.

Ocean colors

Some skates and rays show patterns of color that help them avoid animals that might eat them. Seen from above, dark backs blend in with the dark color of the deep ocean. From below, predators have difficulty seeing light bellies against the brighter, sunlit surface.

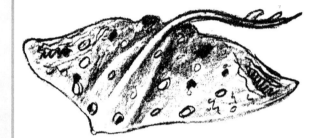

Spines

Some slow-swimming fish, such as the scorpionfish, have sharp or poisonous spines along their backs for protection. A stingray has a poisonous spine on its tail.

The ocean triggerfish gets its name from the first of three stiff spines along its dorsal fin. When it is disturbed, this spine locks upright like a trigger.

Shock treatment

Several fish have special body organs that produce electricity used in defense. The star-gazer has electrical cells in the top of its head. It lies buried in the sand where its electric organ helps it to sense and, if necessary, shock nearby predators.

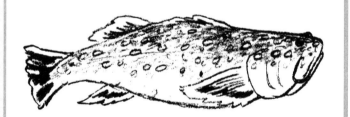

The balloon trick

The puffer fish can inflate its body like a balloon, making it appear larger than it really is. When threatened, the puffer can "blow up" to three times its normal size, too big for many predators to swallow. When the danger is gone, it deflates and swims away.

barbels   the slender bristles on the mouths of certain fish.
dorsal fin   the main fin on the top, or back, of a fish.

Florida Fishes

Flying fish

A fish that can fly? Well, not really, but a flying fish can look like it's flying. It vibrates its long tail in the water until its extended, winglike fins are above the surface, giving the fish enough lift to skim above the water.

It may leave the water at 48 to 64 kilometers (30 to 40 miles) per hour, gliding for 30 seconds and traveling 90 meters (300 feet) before it dives back into the ocean. Flying fish do this mainly to escape from larger fish, such as tuna or dolphin, that eat them.

Don't confuse me with Flipper!

The dolphin, or dorado, is a blue, yellow, and gold fish that should never be confused with the marine mammal that has the same name. The dolphin fish has a blunt forehead and is one of the fastest fishes in the sea, with speeds estimated at more than 80 kilometers (50 miles) per hour!

Bluefish

Bluefish, named for their silvery-blue color, travel in large schools and feed on smaller fish. They have sharp teeth, and if you happen to be in the surf when "the blues are running," you could accidentally be grazed or cut during their feeding frenzy!

Snappers

Snappers are important to Florida fishermen. Although they live mainly in tropical waters, some species are wide ranging. They can grow into very large fish, and often spend their time patrolling the hardbottom, reefs, and wrecks where smaller fish like to hide.

The mutton snapper has a small spot on the side of its pinkish body. It is a prized seafood and is often sold in markets as red snapper.

Life on the Ocean Floor

Some animals, instead of drifting along in the currents or propelling themselves under their own power, live on the ocean floor. These bottom dwellers that slink, slither, and crawl are called benthic animals.

Benthic animals never venture far up the water column. Most of them are dull in color, and some spend their entire lives on, or just beneath, the sea floor. Here, where water movement is weak and no pounding waves or tossing currents can harm their bodies, animals are often quite delicate.

When a swimming animal or a floating seaweed dies, it joins a slow rain of other dead animals, plants, and wastes that drift down to the bottom of the sea. For many benthic animals, this detritus is their main source of food.

Sea cucumbers

Sea cucumbers live on the ocean floor atop the muck or partially buried in it. A sea cucumber looks like a big fat cucumber and feeds on detritus.

A cucumber "breathes" through its rear end, which it keeps exposed above the surface of the sea floor. If it is disturbed, it will sometimes eject its "innards," but luckily for the cucumber, it can quickly regrow them!

Brittle stars

The brittle star is well-named, since its small, flattened body has many long, slender arms that can easily break off. When uncovered from its hiding place in the mud or sand, it moves its arms in snakelike motions, giving it another name, serpent star.

benthic   referring to animals that live on the bottom of the ocean.

detritus   particles of decayed animals and plants.

Animal "flowers"

Anemones belong to the jellyfish and coral group. In its early life, an anemone is a free-swimming planktonic animal. But it spends the adult part of its life as a large polyp, attached to a hardbottom with its tentacles waving to catch prey. If touched, most anemones shrink down into a soft blob.

Just like certain sea jellies, anemones use nematocysts, or stinging cells, to capture plankton or small fish. Some fish, however, can safely live among the stinging tentacles and not be harmed by them. The anemone provides protection and food scraps for the fish, and in turn, the fish lures other creatures into the anemone's tentacles. Both the fish and the anemone benefit from this relationship.

How do we know who lives on the bottom?

An average diver with a scuba tank can dive to only about 60 meters (200 feet). The pressure of the sea water is usually too great for most people to tolerate. How, then, can we know what life is like far below on the sea floor?

Scientists have designed machines called remotely operated vehicles, or ROVs, that are lowered from research ships to the sea floor. Like tethered robots, their specially-mounted television cameras show us the fascinating world of the deep ocean.

polyp   a marine animal with a tubelike body which is attached at one end to a hard surface and which has a mouth at the other end.

Dangers in the Deep

Many sea creatures eat other living animals to survive. An animal that kills other animals for food is called a predator.

Sharks

Sharks are the most well known and feared of the predators. With more than 250 species, the shark family is huge and varied. It includes the plankton-eating whale shark weighing 11,000 kilograms (12 tons) and the tiny, 25-centimeter (10-inch) long, smooth dogfish.

Most sharks are torpedo-shaped and covered with tiny, teethlike scales that make them feel as rough as sandpaper. A shark's powerful tail speeds its streamlined shape through the water.

A shark is both a carnivore and a scavenger. It relies on vision, a keen sense of smell, and an ability to detect movement to find food in murky waters.

Most sharks find food scarce on the bottom. Though they will sometimes rest on the bottom, or swim just above it looking for benthic animals to eat, they may have to eat one another instead, or move hundreds of feet up the water column to find smaller fish to prey upon.

Tiger shark

With stripes like a tiger, this large predator often grows to 4 meters (14 feet) or more. It feeds on all kinds of sea life, including rays and even other sharks.

Unlike certain shark species that lay eggs in leathery cases, the tiger shark gives birth to live young, but the mother does not care for them once they are born.

Smooth dogfish

The smooth dogfish swims in huge schools in shallow waters, searching for sick or injured fish, lobsters, and crabs. Its small teeth grind together to crush the hard shells.

Shark's teeth

A shark constantly sheds worn-out teeth and grows new ones. With three to fifteen sets of teeth neatly arranged in its jaw, a shark may go through as many as 30,000 teeth in a lifetime!

You can find ancient shark's teeth on some Florida beaches. Sizes range from the tiny teeth of the sharp-nosed shark to the hand-sized teeth of the extinct giant white shark.

carnivore   an animal that eats other animals.
scavenger   an animal that feeds on dead animals.

Shark suckers

The remora, or shark sucker, is a fish that attaches itself to sharks or other large fish for a free ride and for any leftover dinner scraps.

Its unusual, oval-shaped suction disc flaps open to create the suction the remora needs to attach to its host.

Look out!

Swimmers and fishermen watch for fins breaking the surface of the water. Each shark species has its own shape of fin, but not all of the fins you see sticking out of the water belong to sharks. Porpoises, dolphins, skates, and rays sometimes show their fins above water.

Skating along

Skates, stingrays, and manta rays all have flat bodies with skeletons made of cartilage (like sharks) and winglike pectoral fins that help them swim gracefully through the water. Most live near the sea bottom, where they feed on shellfish, worms, and crabs.

Manta ray

This huge, harmless ray, as big as a small car, is sometimes called the devil ray. It often rests at the surface with its "wings" barely breaking the water. Sometimes it leaps completely into the air, falling back into the sea with a thunderous slap, almost as if it were playing. Manta rays are common in the warm waters of the Gulf Stream.

pectoral fins a pair of lower fins toward the front of a fish's body.

Marine Mammals

Of all the creatures that live in Florida's offshore waters, the marine mammals—whales, dolphins, and manatees—seem to fascinate us most.

They are warm-blooded animals of the sea that breathe air, have hair, and feed and care for their young. Special adaptations enable them to live in their watery world. Layers of blubber help them cope with cold ocean temperatures, for even around Florida the water is cold in the winter.

Whales and dolphins dive to great depths to capture food. Their bodies are built to survive the pressures of deep water. To communicate with one another, they make unusual sounds by forcing air through closed nasal cavities. They also reflect sounds off the ocean floor, like echoes, to help them find their way through murky ocean waters.

Southern right whale

One of the largest animals in the ocean gets all the nourishment it needs from feeding on the tiniest animals. The gigantic southern right whale strains microscopic zooplankton through huge baleen plates in its mouth. The whale forces water out through the plates to trap food. Then the whale licks the plankton off the baleen with its tongue and swallows it.

The southern right whale is an endangered species that migrates by Florida's Atlantic coast during the winter. A narrow strip of ocean water between Cape Canaveral and the Georgia-Florida border is its only known calving ground.

Long ago when whaling ships sailed the seas, sailors named these animals right whales because they were the "right" whales to kill. They swam slowly, which made them easier to catch, and when they died they floated, which made it easier to tow their carcasses. Even though by international agreement the right whale is no longer hunted by most nations, it still faces the danger of being struck by a ship as it swims along the surface.

baleen plates   horny material that hangs in fringed plates from the upper jaw of certain whales (also called whalebone).
blubber   fatty tissue in whales and their relatives.
calving ground   a place where female marine mammals give birth to their calves. (It's in the water even though it's called "ground.")

mammal   an animal that has a backbone and hair, and that gives birth and cares for its young.
nasal cavities   air passages in the nose.

Bottlenosed dolphin

Some marine mammals use sharp teeth to capture and eat squid and fish. Dolphins and porpoises belong to this group, and many people use these names interchangeably. But most commonly, those species with long beaklike jaws and cone-shaped teeth are called dolphins, while those without a beak and with broad, flat teeth are called porpoises.

There are many species of dolphin, but the bottlenosed dolphin is probably most familiar to us. We see it "surfing" in the bow waves of ships and performing at marine aquariums. Like most marine mammals, it is very intelligent and can memorize tricks and solve simple problems, such as maneuvering though an underwater maze.

The dolphin has a triangular-shaped dorsal fin that looks very much like a shark fin when you see it cutting through the water. But dolphins are a shark's natural enemy in the ocean. When gangs of dolphins ram a shark, one after another, they can chase it away and sometimes even kill it.

bow wave   waves made by the front of a boat.

Ocean Flyers

Seabirds live on or near the sea and get their food from it, either close to the coast or far offshore. They include familiar pelicans, gulls, and terns, as well as lesser-known petrels and gannets.

Although seabirds roam the world's oceans, we have limited knowledge of these far-ranging birds because they usually fly far from the sight of land. Yet the numbers of ocean-going birds stun the imagination. In fact, one of the smallest seabirds, the Wilson's storm-petrel, may be the world's most abundant bird!

Most seabirds have long, narrow wings to help them soar and glide effortlessly over the wave-tossed ocean. Their webbed feet act as brakes and assist in take-offs from the water.

Even though they spend most of their time at sea, they must return to land to raise their families, often gathering in huge colonies. They usually nest on remote islands or rugged cliffs where predators are few.

Storm-petrels

The storm-petrel has long legs in proportion to its small size. It flutters about with its legs dangling and feet pitter-pattering over the waves, as if it were walking on the water.

The storm-petrel belongs to a family of birds known as "tube-noses," because its nostrils extend in tubes along the outside of its bill. Tube-nosed birds get rid of excess salt in their bodies through these nasal cavities, and also use them to sniff out dead floating fish—food—from a great distance.

Gannets

The gannet, a large white and black seabird, flies off Florida's coast during the winter. It can dive from a considerable height, sometimes 30 meters (100 feet) or more, plunging beneath the surface to catch a mackerel or a flying fish in its powerful bill.

The telltale flash of white feathers alerts other gannets to the fishing action, and in no time others join the feeding frenzy. After eating, gannets often rest together on the water in loose flocks called rafts.

Frigatebirds

Not all seabirds catch their own fish. The magnificent frigate-bird, also called the man-o'-war bird because of its warlike thievery, is a pirate who steals its meal from other seabirds.

With a deeply forked tail and long narrow wings that spread to over seven feet, the frigatebird soars and chases other seabirds for their food. It can also snatch flying fish or other food from the surface, but cannot swim or dive. In fact, it quickly becomes waterlogged if it rests on the surface, so the frigatebird must return to land at night to roost.

During the breeding season the male frigatebird inflates a balloonlike red patch of skin on his throat, which certainly must impress any female frigatebird nearby!

raft   a group of seabirds resting on the water.
roost   to rest or sleep on a perch or branch.

Migration and the "Little Guys"

Besides seabirds, which spend their entire lives flying over the world's oceans, other birds cross this vast open space twice each year. Millions of warblers, thrushes, and other songbirds fly high above Florida's offshore waters on their journey between summer nesting grounds in North America and winter homes on Caribbean islands or in Central or South America.

The journey is a difficult one, with the dangers of high winds and storms and the threat of exhaustion from flying nonstop over hundreds of kilometers of open water. Many small songbirds needing a rest find an island, the deck of a ship, or an oil-drilling platform to land on along the way.

Hurricane!

More hurricanes strike Florida than any other state, so it's no wonder that the Florida peninsula has been called "Hurricane Alley."

Hurricanes always form over offshore waters, because they depend on warm ocean temperatures and certain weather conditions. Most of the hurricanes that strike Florida's coast develop far out in the Atlantic Ocean, although some begin in the Caribbean Sea or Gulf of Mexico. How do the animals and plants living offshore deal with these powerful ocean storms?

peninsula   a narrow strip of land jutting into the ocean from the mainland.

Birds in the wind

Most seabirds fly out of the path of a hurricane. However, the violent winds sometimes hurl birds great distances through the air or across the sea.

Some species, such as the smaller and lighter storm-petrels or terns, may be "wrecked" ashore and later discovered wandering about dazed in the streets of inland towns. After a Florida hurricane we often hear reports of birds that have been blown far from their usual territories.

Sea creatures

Fish, whales, and most benthic animals have few problems with violent storms. Those living closer to the surface, however, near the powerful winds and waves, have a greater risk of injury during a hurricane.

In shallow seas, hurricane-spawned waves and currents can scour the sea floor, breaking coral and covering hardbottom communities and seagrass beds with a choking cover of silt and sand. Seaweeds and other marine plants can be torn apart and moved great distances from their original location.

Sea beans, nuts, and seeds from other countries wash ashore on Florida beaches or are blown far inland on the winds of a hurricane, sometimes sprouting in their new location.

Marine Conservation

For the ocean and its wildlife, the damaging effects of natural events such as hurricanes or red tides seem short-lived. But as we learn more about the fascinating world of the sea, we realize that human actions, too, affect the health of the ocean and its plants and animals.

On Florida beaches we find litter either thrown from ships and boats miles offshore or carried by ocean currents from far away. Dolphins and seabirds are caught in abandoned nets, and tangled fishing line traps fish and other animals. Snapper, shrimp, and clams become more difficult to catch each year because of overfishing. Ships and oil-drilling operations spill chemicals into the ocean, polluting the water and poisoning animals.

If we care about the ocean environment, we must be willing to protect Florida's offshore waters through beach cleanups and litter patrols, responsible fishing, and letters to local newspapers and politicians about stopping pollution. What ideas do you have for safe-guarding the sea?

Working together, we can keep the oceans and the creatures that live there alive and healthy so kids in the future also can share in the wonders of the sea.

Glossary

alga (AL-guh)   one of certain plants that usually live in water. The plural — algae (AL-jee) — is used more often.

appendage   an attached body part.

baleen plates   horny material that hangs in fringed plates from the upper jaw of certain whales (also called whalebone).

barbels (BAR-buls)   the slender bristles on the mouths of certain fish.

benthic   referring to animals that live on the bottom of the ocean.

bioluminescence (bi-oh-loom-in-ESS-ins)   light given off by living organisms.

bivalve   an animal with two matching shells hinged together, such as a clam.

blooms   unusually high growths of phytoplankton.

blubber   fatty tissue in whales and their relatives.

bow wave   the waves made by the front of a boat.

brackish   slightly salty.

calcareous (kal-KARE-ee-us)   containing lime, or calcium carbonate.

calving ground   a place where female marine mammals give birth to their calves. (It's in the water even though it's called "ground.")

carnivore   an animal that eats other animals.

cartilage   semi-hard, elastic-like tissue that takes the place of a skeleton in some animals.

colonize   to settle as a group and grow in a new environment.

colony   a group of the same kind of animal living together.

continental shelf   the sea bed surrounding a continent, the edge of which drops steeply to the ocean floor.

detritus (de-TRY-tus)   particles of decayed animals and plants.

dorsal fin   the main fin on the top, or back, of a fish.

ecosystem   communities of plants and animals that naturally grow and live together.

evaporation   changing from a liquid to a vapor.

flagellum (fla-JEL-lum)   a long, hairlike growth from a cell that helps it move.

food chain   the passage of food energy from plants, which make their own food from the energy of the sun, to animals that eat plants, to animals that eat other animals.

hardbottom   rocky areas of the sea floor.

inlet   a narrow waterway opening of the coastline.

invertebrate   any animal without a backbone.

larva (plural: larvae [LARV-eye])   the immature form of an animal that is very different from its adult form.

mammal   an animal that has a backbone and hair, and that gives birth and cares for its young.

marine   in or about the sea.

micro-community   a small, specialized habitat of plants and animals.

microscopic   too small to be seen without a magnifying lens.

nasal cavities   air passages in the nose.

nautical mile   a measurement used in ocean navigation, equal to 1852 meters (6076 feet).

nematocysts (nee-MAT-uh-sists)   stinging cells in the tentacles of coral polyps, jellyfish, and anemones.

nudibranch (NOOD-uh-brank)   a sea slug whose name means "bare gills."

nutrients (NOO-tree-ints)   foods that promote growth.

organic   made of living (or formerly living) plants and animals.

pectoral fins   a pair of lower fins toward the front of a fish's body.

pelagic (puh-LAJ-ik)   referring to the open sea.

peninsula   a narrow strip of land jutting into the ocean from the mainland.

phytoplankton (FIE-toe-plank-ton)   plant plankton.

plankton   microscopic plants and animals that drift in the sea.

polyp (PAUL-lip)   a marine animal with a tubelike body which is attached at one end to a hard surface and which has a mouth at the other end.

porous   having pores, or holes, through which water can flow.

predator   an animal that hunts, kills, and eats other animals.

prey   an animal that is eaten by another animal.

raft   a group of seabirds resting on the water.

refract   to change the direction of a light wave.

roost   to rest or sleep on a perch or branch.

salinity   the amount of salt in the water.

scavenger   an animal that feeds on dead animals.

sedentary   moving about very little.

sessile (SESS-ul)   referring to animals that require something to attach to.

silt   a fine layer of mud and clay.

species (SPEE-sheez)   a kind of plant or animal.

stalked   having a stem.

synthetic   not natural, but man-made by chemical processes.

tentacles   a ring of food-gathering appendages surrounding the mouth of some marine animals.

translucent   allowing light to partially pass through.

vertebrate   an animal with a backbone.

water column   the space from the water surface to the ocean floor.

zooplankton (ZOE-uh-plank-ton)   animal plankton.

Index

Bold page numbers indicate pages where extended information may be found.